Money Guide
Your Home

By the Editors of *Money*

Andrews and McMeel

A Universal Press Syndicate Company
Kansas City/New York

Money Guide: Your Home copyright © 1990 by Time, Inc.
All rights reserved.
Printed in the United States of America.
No part of this book may be used or reproduced
in any manner whatsoever
except in the case of reprints
in the context of reviews.
For information write
Andrews and McMeel,
a Universal Press Syndicate Company,
4900 Main Street, Kansas City, Missouri 64112.

Library of Congress Cataloging-in-Publication Data
Money guide. Your home / by the editors of Money.
p. cm.
"Previously published in magazine format as Money guide:
your home by Money magazine"—T.p. verso.
ISBN 0-8362-2212-1 : $6.95
1. House buying. 2. House selling. 3. Home ownership—Costs.
4. Real estate investment. 5. Real estate business.
I. Money (Chicago, Ill.) II. Title: Your home.
HD1379.M65 1990
643'.1—dc20 90-1112
CIP

The material in this book was previously published in magazine
format as *Money Guide: Your Home* by
Money magazine, a publication of Time, Inc.

ATTENTION: SCHOOLS AND BUSINESSES

Andrews and McMeel books are available at quantity discounts with bulk purchase for education, business, or sales promotional use. For information, please write to: Special Sales Department, Andrews and McMeel, 4900 Main Street, Kansas City, Missouri 64112.

CONTENTS

Foreword

Life, liberty, and the pursuit of a house that rises in value every year without fail. To many Americans, those had become the inalienable rights of citizenship over the past four decades. The 1990s are already different. Just ask sellers in Atlanta. Two years ago, the average house sold 106 days after being placed on the market, often selling just 7 percent below the initial asking price. Now that same house languishes six weeks longer, and chances are the deal closes 10 percent or more off the owner's fond first price. Is a housing bust on the way? Not likely. But getting the greatest value from your biggest investment requires fresh approaches these days. Laying out the latest, smartest strategies—whether you are a buyer, a seller, or an owner looking to make his or her home the best it can be—is the goal of this *Money Guide*.

This guide was put together over four months by a core staff of 25 led by senior editor Richard Eisenberg, *Money* magazine's chief real estate editor. In his 12 years here, Eisenberg has reported, written, or edited more than two dozen features on real estate and housing. But this project took on special significance. "Lately," he reports, "my wife and I have been attending open houses in the New York City suburbs, where we live. We're looking to trade up, and we think now is a great time to buy." Bully for him! But good luck too: he's also got to sell his three-bedroom colonial in Cranford, New Jersey.

Eisenberg's principal editorial aides were associate editor Walter L. Updegrave, a 10-year veteran of real estate reporting, and senior writer Joanna L. Krotz, author of *Metropolitan Home Renovation Style* (Villard Books, $19.95) and, until November of last year, features director of *House Beautiful* magazine.

Chief of correspondents Sian Ballen guided more than 30 reporters in 24 cities who spent an average of 75 hours each interviewing owners and visiting more than 200 homes.

We as journalists hope to present here the liveliest, most accurate and useful guide you'll find anywhere to the new realities of home ownership in the 1990s.

TYLER MATHISEN
Assistant Managing Editor, *Money*

Introduction: The Once and Future House

Joanna L. Krotz

Let's kiss off the '80s: No more trying on houses, showing off the fit, then shedding them to acquire next year's model. Nobody's knocking the dollars such trade-ins and trade-ups generated, but since today's softer markets make fast, profitable turnarounds unlikely, how utterly relieving to choose a place where we can stay put for a while and still feel smart.

What do the houses we want now look like? The answer: In many ways, pretty much as they have for years, but updated with the sophisticated comforts of the present. They have corbels and classical columns, dormers and gables, tiled roofs and whitewashed stucco walls. You know—real houses with familiar architectural details, no matter the size. "We're rebounding from the ideology of modernism," says Robert Olson, a senior associate at the Institute for Alternative Futures, a strategic planning and consulting group in Alexandria, Virginia. "Now there's a shift back to decoration."

Sociology and personal style also dictate home design trends. So when couples like Gene and Martha Dyer made the move to a casual, low-maintenance townhouse in a Georgia retirement village, they spent a hefty $12,000 extra to add a sunroom because, says Martha, "we like to sit there and watch the weather changing through the glass walls and roof."

In the '90s, forecasts William Devereaux, the Washington, D.C., manager of the Berkus Group Architects, "the push will be to create affordable luxury." The need to trade off space versus location and design versus dollars will spark ingenious compromises. James and Sharon Mount, for example, built and maintain their snazzy Florida weekend retreat by sharing the costs with another family.

No doubt, in the '90s, houses will require new discipline and practicality for buyers, sellers, and owners. But the American dream still thrives. All you need is a wish list.

1. The American Dream Revised

Walter L. Updegrave

Homeowners now face a tough new set of house rules in the '90s. By mastering them, you'll become a smarter buyer, happier owner, and swifter—and richer—seller.

The Great American Dream of Home Ownership Is Dead. That dark declaration is what the scare headlines in newspapers and weekly magazines would have you believe. "The Great Housing Bust," thunders *Newsweek.* "Crumbling Castles: Recession in Real Estate," screams *Barron's.* "Shaky Structure: Home-Price Slump Spreads to Both Coasts, Causing Market Jitters," warns the *Wall Street Journal.* Should these ominous rumblings fail to fluster you, consider this bleak house scenario: a widely cited December 1988 study sponsored by the National Bureau of Economic Research, a Cambridge, Massachusetts, think tank, prophesies a 47 percent collapse in housing prices by the year 2007.

Not so fast. If you belong to one of the nation's 58 million homeowning households or aspire to join the club, you will be relieved to know that the doomsayers' predictions are more attention-getting than accurate. Like many specious arguments, though, the house-bust thesis contains a kernel of truth. House prices will probably rise only about 5 percent a year on average in the early '90s, roughly matching or only barely exceeding inflation, and in some years prices won't keep pace at all (see the graph on page 9). That's a far cry from the late 1970s, when annual gains of 12 percent or more routinely left inflation in the dust. And it's certainly no replay of the rapid, 20 percent a year or more price rises that spoiled owners in many housing markets, mostly on or near the coasts, in the second half of the 1980s. Then too, home values in some areas will slide temporarily, much as they have recently slipped 10 to 15 percent in once hot markets such as Boston's and New York City's affluent suburbs. But a bust, with prices crashing 40 to 50 percent coast to coast? "That's impossible unless we see a '30s-style depression," says John Savacool, director of real estate and construction research at the WEFA Group, a Bala Cynwyd, Pennsylvania, economics forecasting firm. "And no one," he says, "is seriously predicting that."

Yet what is inescapably true is that the American Dream—which had become a vision not merely of owning a home but also of having it rise in value year after year, easily outpacing inflation—is rapidly evolving into a new '90s incarnation. In stock market terms, Americans will increasingly regard their homes not as growth investments with huge appreciation potential but as assets that deliver the satisfying total return of moderate price gains plus the joyous dividend of owning a place that reflects one's taste and needs.

Making sure you experience that total return is the goal of this new *Money Guide.* To get a solid start, consider the following seven major housing trends of the '90s, derived from dozens of recent interviews with real estate brokers, builders, furnishings retailers, housing analysts, and demographers:

1. As incomes rise nationally, house prices will appreciate more than in the '80s but less than in the '70s. Perhaps surprisingly, the national median sales price for the typical single-family house, now $94,000, actually fell, after adjusting for inflation, in the past decade. The prices, in 1980 dollars: $62,473 now versus $63,020 then. In the go-go '70s, by contrast, house prices outgunned the consumer price index by an average of almost three percentage points a year. Look for something in between during this decade, with home appreciation rates generally running nose to nose with, or barely edging out, inflation's expected 4.8 percent average annual pace.

2. Though our houses will appreciate less than in some

eras, we will appreciate them more. As 76 million aging babyboomers born between 1946 and 1964 go from career-bent yuppies to sofa spuds with little spudsters, the house will be a nesting place that draws friends and family together. As a result, homeowners will lavish more time and money into making their residences comfy as well as reflective of their personal aesthetics. Says Frederick Elkind, a vice president of TrendSights, a research division of the advertising firm Ogilvy & Mather: "The house will become the ultimate sanctuary and our favorite place to sit on our money."

3. The affordability squeeze is likely to ease. For the first time since the depression, the percentage of U.S. households owning homes has fallen—from 65.6 to 63.9 percent between 1980 and 1988. Yet ownership rates should stabilize this decade and might even inch up. "The two million young people who couldn't buy in the '80s as prices rose faster than incomes will be far better off financially in the '90s," predicts James Brown, director of the Joint Center for Housing Studies at Harvard University. "The babyboomers are in their prime earning years, and they're more likely to be able to afford a home now." At the same time, because of the so-called baby bust of the late '60s and early '70s, there will be fewer Americans in their twenties and early thirties than in the past decade, and those are the ages when people traditionally switch from renting to owning. In all, the number of new young households could decline by 195,000 a year for the first half of the decade. Partly as a result . . .

4. Buyers will gain the upper hand over sellers in many regions and market segments. While prices should perk along nationally, a glut of listings from owners anxious to trade up and a relative dearth of first-time buyers will force some sellers to accept demands for price cuts and the sharing of closing costs. The buyer's sharp new edge will be felt most by owners and builders trying to sell the smaller two-bedroom houses and condos sought by younger people. Some lucky buyers may find themselves in a bargain hunters' paradise as the government's Resolution Trust Corporation—the new agency created by the savings and loan bailout—disposes of its inventory of 11,918 repossessed single-family homes previously owned by insolvent thrifts.

5. Buyers can count on speedier service from lenders—and may enjoy single-digit mortgage rates for much of

the decade. As the 30-something crowd meanders into middle age, economists expect it to start saving madly, boosting the national savings rate (lately just over 5 percent) to 8 percent or so by the mid-'90s. The resulting flood of capital—roughly $40 billion each time the savings rate nudges up one percentage point—would make more money available for borrowers and thus help drive down mortgage interest rates. Says Barbara Allen, housing analyst for the investment firm Kidder Peabody: "By the mid-1990s, I wouldn't be surprised to see fixed-rate mortgages fall to 8 percent and maybe as low as 7 percent." Recent rate: roughly 10 percent. One way mortgage lenders will troll for business will be through fast loan approvals. Already, Citicorp's MortgagePower Plus makes commitments in as little as 15 minutes. The fastest lenders won't necessarily offer the best deals, though. (For more, see "Locking in the Best Price and Financing" on page 32.)

6. Sellers will work harder to unload their houses but will pay brokers less for helping. While homes quickly selling over their listing prices will be about as common as interviews with Salman Rushdie, sellers can take solace in the prospect of lower brokerage commissions later in the decade. A surfeit of real estate agents relative to listed homes—in the late '80s the number of agents rose 6.2 percent while listings *fell* 1.8 percent—is already beginning to squeeze the once standard 6 percent brokers' commission. In the '90s, commissions of 4 percent may become common, predicts John Tuccillo, chief economist for the National Association of Realtors.

7. Environmental concerns will grow for both buyers and sellers. "Environmentalism is no longer kooky. It's mainstream," says Sanford Goodkin, a real estate specialist with the accounting firm KPMG Peat Marwick. Look for buyers to be more attuned to indoor air quality, outdoor noise pollution, and underground water contamination. Says Stephen Martin, executive director of the National Association of Environmental Risk Auditors: "By the end of the 1990s, you may not be able to sell a house or get financing for one unless it's been subjected to rigorous environmental screening."

Generalizing about real estate is tricky, of course, since trends typically diverge by types of homes and regions. Many analysts believe, though, that the huge regional disparities that characterized housing markets last decade—

prices in Houston, for instance, skidded 23 percent from 1983 through 1988 while those in Hartford rose 106 percent—will not recur in the '90s. A slower national economy, growing at roughly 2.2 percent a year compared with 2.4 percent in the '80s, will restrain appreciation. Also, rising shelter costs that have accompanied sizzling housing markets are shutting out prospective buyers and cooling down prices. Even high-flying Orange County, California, is losing altitude as buyers balk at a median house price of $250,000. On the East Coast, Rutgers University demographer George Sternlieb predicts that slow-growth prospects and inflated prices could send New Jersey home values down as much as 12 percent this year.

Meanwhile, yesterday's laggards will catch up as businesses move in to take advantage of their relatively low housing and labor costs. In the Dallas area, for instance, the median home price—which sank 8.6 percent from 1986 through 1988—has since rebounded, rising 7 percent to $93,108 for 1989. The explanation given by local real estate analysts is the hiring of almost 30,000 people last year to staff new or expanded facilities and even headquarters for the like of Fujitsu America, GTE, and J.C. Penney.

Relocating homeowners known as equity bandits, who take their gains out of strong markets (like Los Angeles and San Francisco) and move to more moderately priced ones (like Las Vegas and Seattle), will also help iron out regional price differences. Gorbachev's *glasnost* gambit may inhibit housing-price rises in this decade too. If, as many experts now predict, inflation-adjusted defense spending falls dramatically, price appreciation in some defense-industry-dependent areas (such as St. Louis; Long Island, New York; and Virginia's Arlington and Newport News/Norfolk regions) could slow markedly. Prices might even decline slightly in some pockets of especially hard-hit markets.

While the affordability squeeze will probably lessen for middle-income buyers in this decade, it will by no means disappear. Renters wanting to buy will still be tripped up trying to qualify for mortgages in areas where prices seemingly defy the laws of economic gravity. In San Francisco, for example, only 10 percent of all households now earn enough to snare mortgages for the $269,000 median-price home. Many young people are still likely to have trouble coming up with the cash for down payments and closing costs, says David Seiders, chief economist for the National Association of Home Builders. A mortgage requiring only 10 percent down demands that a buyer bring roughly $17,000 in cash to the closing for the median-price house in a moderate-cost city like Philadelphia, $37,000 for the comparable house in Orange County, California.

To help cash-poor buyers, President Bush has proposed legislation allowing first-time home buyers to raid their Individual Retirement Accounts or Keogh plans for up to $10,000, penalty-free, to make a down payment on a home priced at no more than 10 percent above the area's median. This solution will offer slim relief at best, though, since the median IRA and Keogh account balance for the mere 25 percent of potential young buyers who have them, based on a 1986 Federal Reserve study, is just $4,500. A more likely answer for the young and the cashless will be expanded use of equity-sharing agreements. Typically, in such arrangements, a deep-pockets investor looking for tax deductions gets paired with a home buyer who is light on savings but has enough income to carry a mortgage. The two split the profits when the home is sold.

While demand for small starter homes will shrink, a wave of older, more affluent buyers will trigger a boom in the market for large, luxurious trade-ups. Prices for such homes, says Michael Carliner, an economist at the National Association of Home Builders, could rise a full percentage point more than those of houses overall because of this explosive demand. The urge to splurge can already be seen in the size of the 650,000 or so new homes sold each year. Since 1982, the median new home has expanded in size by 23 percent, from 1,500 square feet to 1,850 square feet. During the 1990s, says Carliner, the desire for roomier digs could easily push the size of the median new home to more than 2,000 square feet. Mini-manses of 3,000 square feet or more could become even more prevalent in wealthy neighborhoods and suburbs.

Though such trade-up homes will be expensive—starting at $200,000 in many spots—the traditional trade-up buyers, ages 35 to 54, should be able to pay the tab. By the end of this century, according to the U.S. Census Bureau, 24 percent of these households will earn $60,000 a year or more in 1985 dollars versus only 14 percent of them in 1986.

Sumptuous move-up houses—or, as more and more owners renovate instead of move, grand additions to existing homes—will probably feature spacious master bedrooms with walk-in dressing suites and enough area for a small home gym. Their lavish bathrooms will sport the like of spas, skylights, and six-foot-long whirlpool baths with marble or ceramic borders. Home offices, many with the look and feel of a cozy library or den, could become *de rigueur.* The luxury house of the '90s will also be more exquisitely furnished, drawing far more than in recent years on antiques and stylish handmade accessories. "People are looking for quality," says consumer trend watcher Frederick Elkind. "They don't want cookie-cutter homes with assembly-line furniture anymore."

Sales and prices of vacation homes could boom too as prosperous 40- and 50-something buyers lusting for leisure and luxury eagerly snap up second homes. That would be a real reversal, because the market for cottages and cabins has been depressed since the Tax Reform Act of 1986 restricted write-offs for their owners. Among the second-home areas that could see the biggest price rises: Virginia Beach, Virginia; San Juan Islands; Washington; and Cape Cod, Massachusetts. That doesn't mean you can bank on the frenzied price run-ups of the '70s. But by homing in on a prime location, your vacation hideaway—like your primary residence—should rack up enough appreciation to make the housing doomsayers recant their crash theories.

FINALLY, A HOME THAT'S A KEEPER

Don't get them wrong: Dennis and Laurel McMahon, 35 and 36, wouldn't trade their experiences as Chicago urban pioneers for anything. Between 1980 and 1988 the couple bought, lovingly rehabbed, and sold two Victorian houses in the city's troubled westside Austin neighborhood, and profited by more than $70,000 along the way. But today, like many Americans who traded their way up the housing ladder in the 1980s and have now found the place they really want, the McMahons are settling down, planning to stay put for a while with daughters Claire, 4, and Fiona, 2. "This," says Dennis, the assistant general counsel for the aviation supplier AAR Corporation, "is our dream house."

Specifically, the place the McMahons so happily call home these days is a nine-room, 4,000-square-foot Victorian showcase in River Forest, a sedate suburb about 10 miles west of downtown Chicago. They moved into it three Februaries ago, paying $238,000. Among the house's many attractions are its sunny southern exposure, which appeals especially to Laurel, a homemaker and gardening enthusiast, and its location just three blocks from the public school Claire will attend this fall.

Forgive the McMahons, then, for feeling as though the housing market had singly blessed them. But it truly has. Real estate brought the couple together in 1978, when Dennis bought a $37,500 one-bedroom condominium in the suburban Oak Park building that Laurel's family owned and she helped manage, while living in one of the condos. After taking an old-homes tour of the Austin area, the couple, who married in 1979, sold their condos for a total of $108,000 and bought a four-bedroom bay-windowed Victorian for a mere $33,500. "I know people who paid that for a car," jokes Dennis. Then, aided by their contractor, Jan Seweryn, the McMahons went about a $20,000 remodeling project, ranging from stripping the interior woodwork to replacing the roof.

Six months after moving in—and before the remodeling dust settled—Laurel and Dennis heard about another Victorian selling four blocks away for $65,000. "We had no intention of moving," says Laurel, "but we could not believe our eyes." While the sprawling, five-bedroom house was falling apart—the heat didn't work, for example—its original five fireplaces were intact. The 75-square-foot attached greenhouse cinched it for Laurel. So the McMahons bought the home upon selling their place for $66,000—a quick $12,500 profit, after subtracting remodeling costs. The couple then proceeded to spend $50,000 rehabilitating the new house, including adding a 12-foot-by-13-foot dance floor for parties.

When Claire was born in 1985, the McMahons started thinking about living in a suburban setting more conducive to raising children. In October 1987, Seweryn tipped them off to the four-bedroom, three-bath place they now own. The couple saw the place as one more chance to get busy. They quickly sold their Austin home for $174,500 and secured a $198,000, 7.9 percent adjustable-rate mortgage on the River Forest house. The McMahons now make monthly mortgage payments of $1,600.

So far, the couple has spent about $60,000 restyling the home, starting with removing the grimy siding and painting the exterior. Mercifully, the wainscoting had been preserved in the formal dining room, but the McMahons needed to re-create much of the wood molding and trim. "We try to play up the old features," says Laurel. "We don't want to make it look like we're living in a Victorian exterior with a '90s interior." Dennis squashes thoughts of rescuing another Victorian. "After this project, I think we've been cured," he says. "We're getting too old for any more massive rehabs."

—Carla A. Fried

A FORECAST FOR PRICES

The median-price existing home will gain value at an average 5.4 percent annual rate between now and 1996, according to the WEFA Group, an economic forecasting firm. That should keep owners ahead of inflation, at 4.8 percent. But housing's edge, say WEFA, will mostly be built this year and next. After that, look for rises in consumer prices to outpace those in housing. Not since 1984—and only seven times in the past 20 years—has that been the case.

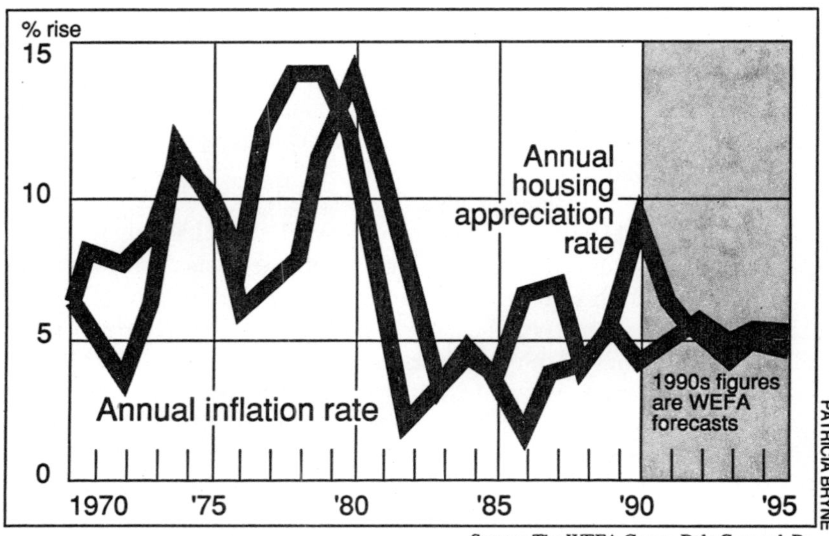

Source: The WEFA Group, Bala Cynwyd, Pa.

2. Finding the Home You'll Really Enjoy

Walter L. Updegrave

In today's squishy markets, you can afford to take your time and get picky, picky, picky.

With FOR-SALE signs seemingly becoming permanent fixtures on more lawns across the country, the balance of power has clearly shifted from home sellers to buyers. As a result, shelter seekers in the buyers' markets of the '90s should be as finicky as Morris the cat. In today's slower-moving markets from Philadelphia to Phoenix, buyers enjoy the luxury of time, and have more houses to choose from than at any time since 1982. Says Amy Twill, regional sales manager of Prudential/Connecticut Realty in Hartford: "The whole atmosphere is more conducive to getting a better deal."

If anything, that's an understatement. These days, you can hold out for the house that precisely suits your taste and needs. Of course, as long as fantasies outstrip incomes, no one can get absolutely everything he's ever dreamed of in one house. There just aren't enough $50,000 waterfront mansions 10 minutes from work to go around. So before beginning any house hunting, even in a sluggish market, you need to decide which features you absolutely must have and which you could compromise on. (Price considerations are a separate matter, as "Locking in the Best Price and Financing" on page 32 explains.)

A thorough investigation of the housing market you're considering will help you focus your search. That's exactly how the McClary family—Bob, a 60-year-old investigator in the county prosecutor's office, his wife Pat, 42, a marketing manager for the Detroit Zoological park, and their 20-month-old baby, Catherine Ann—capitalized on Detroit's dough-boy-soft market last year. The couple diligently scoured various neighborhoods in the city, including Green Acres on the west side and Rosedale Park in northwest Detroit, looking for an area where house values were climbing, homes and yards were well maintained, and a tight-knit sense of community existed. They also kept a mental list of features they required in a home—lots of storage space, a family room, and, most important, a bathroom on the ground floor. "With a baby," says Pat, "you need a place to attend to certain emergencies immediately." After looking at an astonishing 150 houses over 12 months, the couple finally saw one that was just right—a three-bedroom Tudor in the middle-class Warren-Cadieux section on Detroit's east side. They grabbed it for $64,000—$6,000 less than the asking price. "All our work really paid off," says Pat. "This house has everything we want, including a first-floor bath, and it's worth every dime."

Not everyone has to conduct a house hunt with the precision of a Marine drill team. Still, you would do well to emulate the McClarys by mapping out a strategy. Get some professional assistance from a knowledgeable real estate agent. This will save time, since brokers can subscribe to a publication or computer data base known as the multiple listing service; it will have descriptions of all the homes listed in the style and price range you desire. You will find fewer For Sale by Owner ads in today's buyers' markets, anyway; even the most independent-minded sellers recognize the need for professional help when the market stalls. (As the table on page 18 shows, a few cities, such as Chicago, Pittsburgh, and Sacramento, are now sellers' markets where buyers are bidding up prices.)

But with brokers desperate to sell homes today, there's no reason to tolerate one who takes your quest any less seriously than you do. Your broker should, for example, be willing to traipse through as many houses as you want; it's reasonable to look at 10 to 20 listings in one community. Ideally, the broker should also clue you in to upcoming house auctions (for auction-shopping advice, see "Hammer Out an Auction Bargain," page 21). Never forget, though, that when you're ready to make an offer, your broker's allegiance will be to the seller—the person who will be paying him or her the commission out of the sale proceeds.

CHOOSING THE AREA

Before scuffling through a single house, select a few neighborhoods or communities in which to concentrate your search. More than any other factor, the area itself will determine your quality of life and your house's investment potential. Even in Houston, where housing values fell as much as 32 percent from the 1983 market peak, home prices slipped only half as much in top neighborhoods like Tanglewood—and are now rebounding more sharply there. Last year, prices in Tanglewood jumped 30 percent, compared with 11 percent in Houston overall.

Maximize the investment potential of your house by singling out places where housing values are likely to meet or exceed inflation's pace. To identify them, ask a local planning board or economic development office for the area's current employment growth rate. If it is 3 percent a year or more, a steady stream of buyers should keep house-price gains above average.

The areas you shop should also feature the qualities that buyers value most. You can scope out such traits just by driving around: entertainment outlets and access to public transportation and major highways, for example. Others require a little gumshoe work. For instance, to see whether the community has a low crime rate, stop by the police department and find out the level of burglaries and violent crimes in the past year compared with that of other nearby communities of the same size.

A topflight school system is also a strong selling point and certainly a major factor if you have school-age children or soon will. A survey of 4,028 parents by SchoolMatch, a Columbus, Ohio, company that analyzes more than 30,000 U.S. public school systems and private schools, shows that parents prefer schools with classes of 25 students or fewer and per-pupil spending on books, instructional materials, and teachers' salaries that at the very least matches the U.S. average of $4,221. The best systems spend 50 percent more. Surprisingly, most parents do not demand the schools with the highest elementary or high school achievement test scores in the area. Instead, they prefer ones whose students perform at average to above-average levels. William Bainbridge, president of SchoolMatch, says parents would rather have their child be a star at a good school than a mediocre pupil at a superior one.

You can get essential education data for public schools from the state board of education; for private-school information, ask the school's admissions director or headmaster. Get an independent assessment too; for $49, SchoolMatch (800-992-5323; 5027 Pine Creek Drive, Westerville, Ohio 43081) will evaluate a specific public school system or private school against others in neighboring areas or anywhere in the U.S.

Don't judge schools purely by the numbers, though. Meet with principals, and tour facilities. Be sure to ask whether the neighborhood school has the capacity to enroll your child. In some fast-growing areas, local schools are filled to capacity and new kids get bused elsewhere. For example, in Los Angeles, an influx of 15,000 new students last year into the city's already overcrowded largest school district has meant that 24,000 pupils must now be bused to city schools as much as 45 minutes away.

The planning board can fill you in on local issues like land use, business migration, and area environmental hazards—all of which help set house-price trends. By finding out where future business growth will be located, for instance, and then looking for a home in the vicinity, you can "buy in at today's lower prices and sell tomorrow after prices have escalated," advises Peter G. Miller, author of *Buy Your First Home Now* (Harper & Row, $17.95). Just be certain that the locality has a master plan that prevents commercial and industrial development from overwhelming residential areas. Lax zoning regulations can turn a once tidy neighborhood into a cruddy one in a trice.

Press for information about recent developments that could erode home values, such as major employers fleeing the area and taking enough jobs with them to hurt the local economy. Tulsa, for example, lost 28,000 jobs in the early '80s as a result of the oil-price collapse, and its housing market has yet to recover. At $75,223, the average house price last year was 4.4 percent below its 1984 level. New unpopular businesses—a huge mall down the street that might cause traffic congestion, for example—can also dampen housing appreciation. So can environmental dangers such as hazardous-waste dumps or high radon levels (see "Buying the Healthy House" on p. 23).

Sunbelt shoppers especially should ask their agents about the prospective impact on local home values of the Resolution Trust Corporation (RTC)—the federal agency charged with selling off properties once owned by failed thrifts. In hard-hit areas like Austin, RTC-owned houses and condos make up a stunning 11 percent of brokers' inventory. Congress has told the RTC not to unload such properties for less than 90 to 95 percent of their appraised value. But real estate analysts such as Robert Emrich, vice president of the Greenman Group, a Hollywood, Florida, consulting firm, worry that appraisals might have to be lowered to sell these houses. If that happens, people who bought earlier might see their homes drop in value. Beware of areas where the RTC might unload acres of raw land for below-market prices too. Such sales could enable builders to erect new, inexpensive homes and undercut appreciation on existing residences.

Commuting time will also play a major role in dictating where you live. Let your tolerance for traffic—or lack of it—be your guide. If you're a confirmed Type A who needs beta blockers to get through the daily rush hour, you'll live better and longer in a house or condo near work. But if you think of highway driving or a commuter train trip as a chance to mull over business ideas—or take a Walkman break—you may be a candidate for an hour-or-longer commute to a big house and yard in the boonies. To gauge commuting time accurately, don't rely on the broker's estimate. "Make the commute yourself," says Liz Merrill, a broker in Burlington, Vermont. "And do it during peak rush hour—not in midday when traffic tends to be lighter."

Since property taxes in many places can easily run $200 a month on a $150,000 house, you should compare tax bills on homes that interest you with those on others in the area. Remember, you're not interested in what the current owner is paying but what you will owe once you move in. To find out how to calculate what your taxes will be, call local assessors. This nugget is especially important to know these days when cash-strapped legislatures and municipalities are raising property taxes faster than you can say Howard Jarvis.

CHOOSING THE HOME

Once you've winnowed your choices down to a few neighborhoods, start house hunting. Keep in mind that for resale potential, detached single-family houses on lots of one-quarter to one-half acre are hands-down favorites for most buyers. In a 1989 *Builder* magazine survey of 2,025 new-home shoppers nationwide that included singles, couples, and couples with children, at least two-thirds of the buyers in each group preferred a detached house to a townhouse or condominium.

An attached house doesn't necessarily doom you to meager appreciation, though. Some markets are now so expensive that shoppers must bend their preferences to their budgets. In parts of Southern California, for example, detached single-family home prices have climbed so high—often $350,000 or more—that even a trade-up buyer armed with cash from the sale of a smaller home can rarely afford them. As a result, builders have come up with a new type of housing: attached move-ups. These are basically large townhouses with grand and glitzy kitchens and baths costing $150,000 to $300,000. Yet that is still 15 to 20 percent less than detached homes of comparable size and quality.

Think about how much time, energy, and money you'll want to commit to home maintenance and repairs. If you don't keep your home in superior condition, it could be a tough sell when you're ready to move out. Houses built before the 1950s may have more character than freshly built ones, but they require greater care too; houses more than seven years old often cost $1,500 or so a year to maintain, versus a few hundred dollars for younger ones.

If you want the joys of home ownership without much of the drudgery—and are willing to forgo some privacy and potential appreciation—consider a condo or a home in a cluster development, where the condominium or homeowners association maintains the exterior of your house and the common grounds for around $100 a month. Or concentrate on developments still under construction. Don't be taken in by a shiny veneer, however. To check the quality of the builder's materials and workmanship, interview people who bought homes from him within the past year. Also, call the local Better Business Bureau and see whether any complaints have been filed against the builder. You might want to find a builder whose homes come with an insured warranty at no additional fee to you. This policy will cover losses due to faulty electrical, plumbing, and heating and cooling systems within two years and major structural defects within 10 years.

As for style, you will appeal to the largest number of potential buyers when you eventually sell if you stick with houses that are more ordinary than daring. That means, for example, passing up a $500,000 house in a $200,000 neighborhood. A 2,000-square-foot, four-bedroom house with virtually no backyard might also be a tough sell someday since the typical buyers for such a home—families with children—usually want a large lot. You should be especially chary of falling for custom-built homes with avant-garde architecture, because potential buyers who share your preferences may ultimately be harder to find.

Take care to choose a house whose architectural style adds to its value. Increased mobility has widened the range of acceptable styles—good ol' boys in Houston are now buying that old Texas standby, the English Tudor—but regional preferences can still run strong. In New England, for example, ranch-style houses are as popular as Ceausescu posters in Bucharest and thus could become a tough sell for you someday.

It's important, of course, to be certain that a home's layout fits the way you really live. Families with small children, for example, often prefer a kitchen that opens onto the family room, so Mom or Mr. Mom can keep an eye on the kids while preparing meals. Parents should also be mindful of traffic patterns within the house. No, not special lanes for little Mikey's Big Wheel, but the route you must take to get from room to room. Ideally, in a household with young kids, the family room should be well clear of the formal dining room where you will entertain adult friends. Parents of teenagers often prefer that the master bedroom be placed as far away from their kids as possible—preferably on the opposite side of the house—to save them from 40-decibel renditions of such tunes as Guns 'n' Roses' raucous hit "Welcome to the Jungle."

You may also need a room that's not found in every home. For instance, a household with a grandparent or a boomerang child—one who moves back in after college, a divorce, or a job layoff—may prefer a house with an accessory apartment and a separate entrance. Dual-career couples may find a home office to be indispensable.

Finally, with so many places to choose from, don't be afraid to let comfort help you select a home. Why settle for spartan amenities when you can find sumptuous splendor? Go ahead, live it up. Luxe features like French doors, clerestory windows, and cathedral ceilings will make your house brighter and more livable, and will probably add value. The same goes for large kitchens with top-quality cabinets and walk-in pantries. Ditto spacious bathrooms with dual lavatories, oversize tubs, and separate showers. Feathering your nest in the '90s not only will make your time at home more enjoyable, but also should make it easier to find an eventual buyer when you're ready to fly.

TOMORROW'S HOT AND COLD MARKETS

Until now, Sacramento was famous largely for its tomato juice and a lamentable pro basketball team. But as the table on the next page shows, California's capital could soon become the king of U.S housing appreciation, with home prices rising 7.8 percent this year and a toal of 60.1 percent through 1995 *after* adjusting for inflation. That's the prediction of the WEFA Group, the Bala Cynwyd, Pennsylvania, economic forecasting firm. WEFA analyzed price-gain (and -loss) prospects for resales of single-family houses in the 50 largest U.S. metropolitan areas. Then we subtracted WEFA's estimate of future U.S. inflation rates—4.1 percent in 1990 and 32.6 percent through '95.

According to WEFA, after deducting inflation, the median-price U.S. home will rise in value by 4.5 percent in 1990 versus 1989's slim 0.3 percent gain. Reason: many smaller areas, hit hard by last year's slowing economy, are ready to rebound. Most of the 50 largest markets won't score as well this year, since they'll still be shaking off the housing blahs. The forecast for those metro areas is brighter, though, for the 1990–95 period. WEFA says that fully 37 of the 50 biggest markets will get cumulative postinflation gains exceeding the U.S. average, which the firm pegs at a modest 5.2 percent. That translates to an average annual return (after inflation) of about 0.9% compounded.

The strongest markets will generally be midsize cities with diversified economies. In addition to Sacramento—which is drawing migrants from San Francisco, 90 miles

Metropolitan area	1989 median sales price	Annual income required for buyers*	1989 inflation-adjusted appreciation rate	Projected inflation-adjusted appreciation rate 1990	Projected inflation-adjusted appreciation rate 1990–95
Sacramento	$110,492	$37,200	+11.8%	+7.8%	+60.1%
Pittsburgh	66,681	22,500	+ 0.7	+7.8	+50.2
Portland, Oreg.	70,112	23,600	+3.9	+3.8	+33.2
Boston	183,205	61,700	-3.7	+2.4	+28.8
Memphis	78,160	26,300	-2.7	+1.3	+26.1
Anaheim	246,267	83,000	+14.1	+1.9	+24.0
Tampa/ St. Petersburg	72,838	24,500	+7.0	+4.3	+22.8
Chicago	107,216	36,100	+4.5	+5.0	+22.5
Riverside, Calif.	124,130	41,800	+12.2	+3.6	+22.0
Buffalo	72,322	24,400	+4.9	+2.8	+20.8
Fort Lauderdale	85,857	28,900	+0.9	+4.8	+20.5
Orlando	81,413	27,400	-2.0	+3.4	+20.3
Indianapolis	71,352	24,000	+3.6	+3.1	+19.7
Denver	85,604	28,800	-0.7	+4.5	+19.5
Hartford	167,124	56,300	-5.2	+0.3	+19.4
Miami	86,387	29,100	+0.2	+1.6	+18.9
Monmouth/Ocean Counties, N.J.	162,929	54,900	+2.5	+4.5	+18.7
Kansas City	71,389	24,100	-3.8	-2.0	+17.2
Detroit	74,614	25,100	-3.4	+2.9	+17.0
San Jose	214,136	72,200	+10.1	+1.9	+16.7
Baltimore	96,628	32,600	+4.5	+3.3	+15.7
Washington, D.C.	144,259	48,600	+3.9	+2.1	+15.6
Middlesex/Somerset Counties, N.J.	174,719	58,900	+5.8	-0.3	+14.3
Columbus, Ohio	78,673	26,500	+3.9	+4.4	+13.9
Newark	200,370	67,500	+3.6	+4.1	+13.4
Los Angeles	217,629	73,300	+16.8	+3.0	+12.8
Salt Lake City	69,780	23,500	-1.7	+1.7	+12.0
Oklahoma City	54,073	18,200	-8.9	+3.1	+11.2
San Francisco/ Oakland	262,763	88,500	+20.1	+2.1	+11.1
Long Island	163,905	55,200	+3.6	+2.4	+9.0
Houston	68,504	23,100	+6.3	+2.9	+8.5
Cincinnati	77,258	26,000	+5.9	+2.8	+8.0
Philadelphia	107,700	36,300	-0.1	+0.7	+7.4
San Diego	174,638	58,900	+14.0	+1.5	+7.0
Bergen/Passaic Counties, N.J.	190,269	64,100	-2.1	+0.5	+6.8
Seattle	107,377	36,200	+13.1	+1.8	+6.4
Milwaukee	79,489	26,800	+2.1	+0.5	+5.9
Rochester, N.Y.	78,849	26,600	-0.5	+1.2	+5.2
Norfolk/ Newport News	97,710	32,900	-5.0	-2.2	+4.1
Nashville	81,445	27,400	0.0	+1.9	+3.9
San Antonio	65,384	22,000	-4.1	+3.9	+3.9
Atlanta	82,941	28,000	-1.8	+0.5	+3.8
Minneapolis/ St. Paul	87,338	29,400	-2.9	+0.2	+3.3
Cleveland	75,659	25,500	+4.7	+3.2	+3.0
Phoenix	79,046	26,600	-6.3	-2.4	+2.8
Dallas/ Fort Worth	93,108	31,400	+1.9	+1.0	+2.3
Charlotte, N.C.	89,625	30,200	+5.4	+3.0	+1.2
New York City	183,137	61,700	-7.8	-1.7	-2.2
St. Louis	77,530	26,100	-5.2	-2.3	-3.1
New Orleans	70,677	23,800	-8.2	+0.8	-10.8
U.S. median	$94,019	$31,700	+0.3%	+4.5%	+5.2%

*Gross income needed to buy the median home assumes a 20 percent down payment, a 10 percent, 30-year fixed-rate mortgage, and that the buyer's mortgage equals 25 percent of gross income. Source: the WEFA Group.

southwest, where prices are about 138% higher—WEFA predicts solid profits for owners in Pittsburgh and in Portland, Oregon. But WEFA expects home prices to decline, after factoring in inflation, in New York City, St. Louis, and New Orleans. Times will be particularly tough in the Big Easy, where flat oil prices, stalled employment, and scant income growth may cut house prices by nearly 11 percent by 1996.

—Carla A. Fried

SOLVING THE COMMUTING QUESTION

For many buyers, the perfect house at the right price is the one that best answers this two-part question: How far from work are you willing to live, and precisely what will you trade—in money, space, time, or quality of life for you and your family—to blend the commute with the life you want? There are, of course, as many correct answers to the commuting question as there are home buyers. But finding the right balance for you and your family can be tricky. As the following profiles of recent home buyers demonstrate, it almost always involves compromises.

Living on the Office Doorstep

Solutions to the commuting question may well be toughest for homeowners with children and working spouses. But that's not to say that single people like Daniel Coleman, 26, of San Ramon, California, don't wrestle with commuting's tradeoffs. For Coleman, though, the decision on how to balance daily travel time with housing space and cost came comparatively easily: "When I'm not working," says the trim and courtly bachelor, "I want to *live!* What's the point of commuting to a bigger home if you're never there?"

Thus when his employer, Pacific Bell, transferred the engineer from Sacramento to a major center in San Ramon last April, Coleman knew he wanted a place close to work. He ended up with one—a compact one-bedroom condominium in a two-story development—that's only a five-minute drive from his office. Cost: $96,700, roughly the top price he felt he could swing on his $42,000 annual salary. After putting down 10 percent and taking out an $87,000 adjustable loan at 9.25 percent, his total monthly housing expenses come to $935.

Coleman's solution to the commuting question was inspired in large part by his desire to make time for such pursuits as basketball and weightlifting. Then too, he wanted to minimize commuting's wear and tear on his prized possession: a flashy red 1985, 220-hp Pontiac Trans Am V8. "If I didn't live right near work," he says, "the terrible freeway traffic might kill my engine."

Convenience wasn't Coleman's only consideration, however, in choosing his place. He took price-gain potential into account as well. Ever since companies like Chevron and AT&T started locating major facilities in or near San Ramon in the mid-1980s, crowding out the region's pear and walnut orchards, house prices have taken off—up 25 percent in 1989 alone. Says Coleman: "I figured I'd make more money on this condo near work than on an even bigger place in a community where prices aren't going up so fast."

Coleman knows his bachelor pad isn't forever, but it suits him fine right now. "Maybe when I'm older and I have a family I'll commute the way everyone else at work does," he says. "But for now I'm glad I don't have to."

Buying into a Fuller Life

"I have paid my dues." That's how Susan Drew, a 42-year-old graphic artist, thinks of the five years that her family spent living in Leicester, an isolated town (pop. 870) in central Vermont. Disappointed with Leicester's public schools, Susan and her electronics engineer husband, Charles, 33, even paid $6,400 last year to enroll their eight-year-old twins, Sybil and Sarah, in a neighboring system. Then last summer the Drews decided to move to a more lively world. They sold their chalet-style house for $95,000 and moved 50 miles north to comparatively bustling South Burlington (pop. 12,675), where they bought a brand-new, four-bedroom colonial for $136,900. Never mind that Charles' commute to the Dowty Electronics plant in Brandon, where he manages testing and quality control, went from 10 minutes each way to 60—and that's on good days. On snowy roads, the trip can take 90 minutes, not counting the 15 he devotes to shoveling the driveway and warming up the car. But for the Drews, Charles included, the tradeoffs have been worth it.

Start with the schools. Susan raves about the teachers and the arts programs. Then there are the recreational and cultural opportunities afforded by such attractions as 125-mile-long Lake Champlain and the Burlington area's six colleges, including the University of Vermont. As for the commute, Charles expresses some disappointment about spending less time with his family than he once did, but on balance he is unfazed: "A lot of my job is thinking work that I can do in the car." He often dictates en route and puts his cellular phone to good use, including calling corporate headquarters in Cheltenham, England.

The couple spent five months investigating the tight Burlington housing market—prices have risen 30 percent over the past three years—to find a home worthy of the commute. Their house sits on a quiet circle in a 52-home development where the twins can play safely. Susan says she is especially pleased with the natural gas heating system, after tending a wood-burning stove in their 25-year-old, three-bedroom former house. Her husband enjoys the home for one more reason: "Now we won't have to live with the endless deer season gunfire almost in our backyard."

—Holly Wheelwright

HAMMER OUT AN AUCTION BARGAIN

Roughly one of every 30 houses sold this year—nearly 133,000 in all—will be moved at auction. The comparable ratio just five years ago: a scant 1 in 100. The swift rise should be no surprise. In these days of spottier housing markets, all sorts of impatient sellers—including banks and government agencies peddling foreclosed properties, builders with inventory backlogs, and even individuals—are using auctions to unload attractive houses and condos. The buyer's break: up to 25 percent off the appraised value. But to pocket a genuine jewel instead of overpriced junk, a methodical approach is a must.

Watch for auction ads in your local paper. Then go to the auction company's office to get the bulky bidder's package—typically a 30- to 40-page document setting out, among other things, the terms of the auction, the suggested opening bid, and the details of the homes. During your visit, ask the following questions:

Which bidding method will be used? There are two types: In an **absolute auction,** there's no turning back for the seller; the property goes to the highest bidder no matter how low the final offer is. So-called **reserve auctions** either set a minimum acceptable price or let the seller decide within 48 hours whether to take the highest bid. In either case, bids are normally made aloud, sometimes raucously. Obviously, you stand a better chance of finding bargains at absolute auctions. On the other hand, novices can easily overpay at such auctions if they assume that any purchase is a steal.

Is financing available? Often it is. Some developers auctioning houses extend financing terms favorable enough to land you a home you otherwise couldn't afford. For instance, the 46 Vista, New York, condos auctioned in December with the developer KJB came with 8.5 percent, 30-year fixed-rate mortgages. The catch: buyers had to close on the $106,500-and-up homes within five days.

How must I pay if my bid is accepted? Typically, at the auction you have to hand over earnest money in the form of a certified check for 5 to 10 percent of the suggested opening bid. Usually, you have 45 to 60 days to make the rest of the down payment, secure a mortgage, and close. Since speed is essential, you might want to line up financing in advance by telling a local lender what you anticipate paying and filling out an application. Cost for this service: $85 to $150.

Before you do anything, however, pin down the market value of the homes that interest you, advises Steven Good, president of Sheldon Good & Company, a nationwide auction firm. "If you go to an auction and others are bidding up the property higher than you think it's worth," says Stephen Martin, president of the Gwent Group, a Bloomington, Indiana, consulting firm for auctioneers, "either you haven't done your homework properly—or they haven't." Ask your real estate agent what comparable homes sold for recently. Also, pay a home inspector $150 to $300 to check the house and report back to you. (For tips on hiring a home inspector, see "Inspect Before You Buy," p. 29) Then, still before the auction, ask an attorney to review the prospective contract. If the two of you want to amend it, you'll need to get the seller's approval before the auction. A buyer usually must sign the contract as soon as the auctioneer hollers "Sold!"

—Christina B. Schlank

3. Buying the Healthy House

Andrea Rock

To safeguard your health as well as your home's market value, be sure to perform a rigorous checkup before you buy.

Shortly after a geothermal energy plant began operating eight years ago within three miles of her two-bedroom home in Leilani Estates, a subdivision on the Big Island of Hawaii, Sheila Darsey began experiencing a constant aching in her lungs and painful sinus headaches. She wasn't the only one suffering the ill effects that her doctor believes are caused by hydrogen sulfide emissions from the facility. Her two sons, Cayce, 8, and Kirk, 6, as well as other children in the neighborhood, were plagued by bronchitis and sinus ailments. The family's symptoms cleared up recently when the plant shut down the geothermal well nearest their home. But the reprieve is temporary; more wells are being planned.

Darsey, a 44-year-old carpenter, would gladly move, but negative publicity about the plant has pushed down property prices roughly 30 percent over the past few years. Even if she could find a buyer—two years ago the house sat on the market for six months without a single offer—an appraiser told her the place would fetch maybe $53,000 tops, compared with $150,000 or so for comparable homes in similar but unaffected neighborhoods. "I can't buy anywhere else with that kind of money," says Darsey. "I'm a prisoner in my own home."

As Sheila Darsey discovered firsthand, environmental

hazards can imperil your family's health—and wealth. Because of that, giving a house and its environs a thorough going-over for potential health hazards ranging from cancer-inducing radon gas to high moisture levels that may lead to respiratory problems is now a crucial step in buying any home. Already, mortgage lenders increasingly require that appraisers take such dangers into account in determining the market value of a home. If a problem is severe enough—a house sits near a toxic-waste dump, for example—banks may simply refuse to finance the deal.

To conduct a diagnostic review of any house you are seriously considering, start by hiring a home inspector (see page 29). But to identify a nonstructural problem like contaminated soil, you may have to find a specialist such as an environmental engineer who'll charge $75 to $150 an hour to test for trouble. Don't reject a house simply because it may pose a health problem. Many hazards are not life threatening, and those that are can often be eliminated relatively inexpensively.

Many hazards are common to homes today and pose risks to health. Below you'll find advice on how to detect the problems and what it costs to correct them. Although headline-grabbing threats such as radon and toxic waste carry dire consequences, in most parts of the country your house is likelier to be afflicted by more mundane woes such as poor ventilation and excess moisture. For that reason, we discuss the dangers in descending order from most to least common.

INADEQUATE VENTILATION

"A good ventilation system that gets rid of stale air indoors and brings in fresh air from outside is one of the most critical elements in making your home healthy," says John W. Spears, a building consultant for Geomet Technologies in Germantown, Maryland. To rid the house of harmful pollutants, install a central exhaust fan in the attic or basement. The fan should be vented to the bath, laundry, and kitchen, where moisture buildup can cause mold. An exhaust-fan system, including ductwork for proper venting, costs $300 to $400 if it is put in as the house is built. Installing such a system in an existing house, however, can easily run $1,000. If that price seems too steep, put separate fans in each bathroom and, over the stove, an exhaust hood vented to the outside. Cost: $50 to $100 per installation.

EXCESS MOISTURE

In today's well-insulated homes, moisture from cooking and bathing can easily accumulate and cause respiratory problems. High humidity can also damage a home's structure, causing rot in walls, roof rafters, and sheathing. You can avoid moisture buildup by keeping the relative humidity in your home between 30 and 50 percent. To do that, attach a humidistat, which costs just $30 or so, as a control for the exhaust fan in your ventilation system. This way, the fan automatically pulls moisture from the house when humidity rises above the desired level.

COMBUSTION GASES

If your home has gas-, oil-, or wood-burning appliances, including furnaces—as roughly 70 percent of homes do—be sure that combustion byproducts such as carbon monoxide, nitrogen dioxide, and moisture are being vented outside the home. Start by examining the furnace. If the area around the flue pipe that connects the furnace to the chimney is black, backdrafts may be allowing gases to seep into your house. This problem stems from an inadequate supply of air to the furnace area. Installing an air-intake vent to the furnace, at a cost of $100 or so, will usually correct it.

If you have a wood-burning stove, make sure the door to the combustion chamber fits snugly. You can also prevent gases from escaping into the house by installing air-intake ducts in wood-stove fireboxes and fireplaces. Cost: about $100.

POOR WATER QUALITY

Whether your water is from a municipal supply or a private well, you should have it tested for radon, pH and calcium levels, iron, bacteria, microorganisms, organic substances such as pesticides, and inorganic chemicals such as lead or arsenic. A national mail-order testing service recommended by consumer groups is WaterTest Corporation of America (800-426-8378). To test for all these contaminants, expect to pay about $190 for a kit that tells you how to take samples and interpret the results.

Lead or radon in your water is probably the most perilous problem you may encounter. Lead can leach into the water from lead solder in copper pipes. To solve leaching from lead solder, which was banned as a plumbing material in 1986, install a reverse-osmosis water treatment system that rids your water of lead and other impurities like bacteria and calcium. A model such as the Everpure Ultimate 1 that fits discreetly under a sink sells for around $825 including installation.

If your water comes from a well, radon—the odorless gas identified by the Environmental Protection Agency as the second leading cause of lung cancer after smoking—can enter the water underground and then be released in the air inside the house. An activated-carbon system, which costs about $200, will eliminate this hazard.

FORMALDEHYDE

The two greatest household sources of this toxic chemical are particleboard subflooring—prevalent in houses built since the mid-1960s—and urea-formaldehyde insulation. To check the subfloor, pull up the carpet or a floorboard in a closet and look for boards made of glued wood chips and flakes. You can spot the insulation by checking the attic perimeters or behind electric-outlet cover plates for a telltale light-brown foamy mass or powder. To reduce emission from particleboard, apply two coats of sealant such as Deft Clear Wood Finish, available in hardware stores for about $32 a gallon. There is no practical way to completely seal off vapors from urea-formaldehyde insulation. Removing it is prohibitively expensive, as the material lies between exterior and interior walls. Since the peak levels of vapor are released in the initial years, avoid any house that has had this insulation installed in the previous four years.

LEAD PAINT

Lead paint was used in about two-thirds of houses built before 1940, about one-third built from 1940 to 1960, and even in a few built after 1960. Some state health or housing departments will test houses for lead paint at no charge. If it turns up, take action. Cover cracked or peeling paint with wallpaper or drywall. Doors and moldings should be removed and sent out to be chemically stripped. Any removal done on-site should be performed by trained professionals to reduce the amount of harmful lead dust. Ridding an entire house of lead paint can cost from $5,000 to $15,000. To get names of qualified removal services, call your city or state health department.

ASBESTOS

This cancer- and lung-disease-causing substance is usually found in the insulation surrounding pipes or hot-water heaters and in textured ceilings in houses built from 1900 through the early 1970s, when publicity about its ill effects forced it off the market. If you spot a substance you suspect is asbestos—a chalky cardboardlike material—contact a lab about how to take a sample for testing. Expect to pay $40 to $50. If the asbestos is not crumbling, says Joseph Lstiburek, a building scientist in Chicago, leave it alone. If it is crumbling or you plan alterations that will disturb it, remove or seal the hazard. To avoid getting ripped off by sleazy companies that charge as much as $10,000 to rid your house of this substance, call the local office of the EPA for the name of a trustworthy professional.

PESTICIDES

When misapplied, pesticides used to kill termites and other insects can seep inside, leaving toxic residues that can linger for years. The most dangerous are chlordane, heptachlor, aldrin, and dieldrin—chemicals now banned as termite treatments but used as recently as 1988.

Before making an offer on a home, get a history of pesticide use from the sellers. To determine the risks of a particular substance, call the EPA's pesticide hotline at 800-858-PEST. If you discover that the house was treated within the past 10 years with chlordane or any other banned pesticide, you'd be wise to pass on the place entirely, says Debra Lynn Dadd, a Mill Valley, California, author and consultant who conducts environmental reviews for home buyers. Dadd also advises rejecting a home if it has been treated more than three times during the past 10 years with any termite pesticide.

RADON

Scientists believe that the risks from this radioactive gas, which is produced by the natural breakdown of radium in soil, are serious enough that you should test any house you're considering. The substance is thought to be found at levels high enough to cause cancer in about 10 percent of U.S. homes. For a rough estimate, buy a so-called charcoal-type test kit, such as Air Chek. To get a kit call 800-247-2435; the $9.95 price includes analysis and postage. The EPA has not determined an acceptable level of exposure, but Linda Mason Hunter, author of *The Healthy Home: An Attic to Basement Guide to Toxin-Free Living* (Rodale Press, $21.95), suggests taking action if the level exceeds two picocuries per liter of air, the equivalent of smoking about three cigarettes a day. If the test registers two to 20 picocuries, then before you buy the house, get a cost estimate of bringing the radon level below the two-picocurie level. Your best source for such estimates is radon-reduction specialists. If the reading is higher than 20, don't buy until you get a more accurate reading from an alpha-track detector or electret-ion chamber, which measures radon levels over a three- to 12-month period.

Lowering the radon concentration in a home may be as simple as spending $200 to caulk and seal cracks in the basement walls and around the ceiling of the top floor of the house. But an older house with concentrations of 100 picocuries or more may require adding a subslab ventilation system—a set of pipes inserted into the foundation and vented to the outdoors—at a cost of $1,500 or more. To avoid disreputable contractors, use only radon-reduction specialists listed with your local EPA office.

TOXIC WASTE

Soil or ground-water contamination from toxic-waste dumps or underground storage tanks should be among your foremost concerns in evaluating a homesite. If a house is within one mile of a dump or has fill dirt that came from an old landfill, the soil may be contaminated with toxic matter. Two major risk sources: radioactive refuse from dentists' offices and PCBs (polychlorinated biphenyls), which are cancer-causing agents found in discarded transformers and batteries. To find out whether a home or land is near a dump or has fill dirt from one, check at your local public health office. To test the soil, contact the agriculture department of a nearby university or hire an environmental engineer. Such professionals are listed in the Yellow Pages and typically charge $75 to $150 an hour.

Abandoned underground heating-oil tanks also pose a danger. Your best clue: a pipe sticking out of the ground near the house or in the backyard. For advice on how to eliminate this toxic risk, call the EPA at 800–424–9346.

Reporter associate: Amal E. Morcos

RESOURCES

For more help in your quest for a healthy home, check out these sources:

► *The Healthy House Catalog* (Environmental Health Watch and Housing Resource Center, $19.95 plus $3 shipping; 800-222-9348). A directory of sources for test kits, services, equipment, and building materials.

► *The Nontoxic Home: Protecting Yourself and Your Family from Everyday Toxics and Health Hazards* by Debra Lynn Dadd (J.P. Tarcher, $9.95).

► For the following free pamphlets published by the U.S. Environmental Protection Agency, write to the Public Information Center, 401 M St., S.W., Washington, D.C. 20460: *Radon Reduction Methods—A Homeowner's Guide; Lead and Your Drinking Water; A Citizen's Guide to Pesticides.*

INSPECT BEFORE YOU BUY

The 18-foot cathedral ceiling in the master bedroom hooked you on the house. But how sure are you that those romantic rafters won't come crashing down during the next storm—or that the heating and plumbing systems won't fail 10 minutes after you move in?

Whether you know it or not, you need a home inspector. For $150 to $300, an inspector will check out the plumbing, heating, and electrical systems and scrutinize your home for structural defects.

But finding one who's capable and reputable takes homework. Start your search in the Yellow Pages under "Building Inspection Services." Demand someone who has been doing inspections in your area for at least three years and who can furnish references from a minimum of four customers.

Membership in the American Society of Home Inspectors, a professional organization whose members have completed at least 250 paid inspections, is also a plus. To get names of ASHI inspectors in your area, call 202-842-3096. Make sure the inspector carries liability insurance, which can reimburse you for damages he fails to detect.

Accompany the inspector during his tour and ask questions. Don't expect him to tell you whether you're getting the house at a good price. Although the inspector may estimate repair costs—and you should factor those into any offer—he should *never* solicit work for himself or others. "If the inspector claims you have $5,000 worth of roof damage and then shows you his roofing license," says John Heyn, an inspector in Baltimore, "find another inspector."

A thorough inspection should cover at least the following items:

Structural components. The inspector should check for water stains or cracks that could indicate damage in walls, floors, and the roof. He should also examine window casings, doors and frames, stairs, and the attic for signs of structural damage.

Electrical system. Safety is the chief issue here. The inspector should examine the main electrical panel for aluminum circuit wiring that could cause fires and also see whether outlets are firmly attached to walls and properly grounded. If the house has a fuse box, he should make sure that the fuses have the proper amperage. Otherwise, an electrical fire could occur.

Plumbing. Fixtures such as toilets and sinks should be in working order. He should also check for adequate water pressure and signs of leaks.

Heating and cooling. He should see that the systems deliver adequate heat, cooling, and air flow to all rooms.

Foundation and basement. He'll look for cracks and signs of water seepage in basement and foundation walls that could signal structural damage.

Most inspectors will also test for radon, asbestos, or formaldehyde, gauge the quality of your drinking water and make sure the septic tank is operating properly. The cost: $50 to $100 per test. To check for termites and other wood-destroying pests, hire a termite inspector, who'll probably charge less than $100.

—A.E.M.

WHAT $150,000 BUYS TODAY

$150,000 can still turn the key on comfortable housing in most parts of the country and on spacious, even luxurious digs in some regions. Here is a look at 10 homes, each of which recently sold for roughly $150,000.

► **Raleigh Charmer.** A 4-BR, 1½-BA, 2-deck colonial, only 2 yrs. old. In the up-market western suburb of Cary, N.C. Skylights in master bedroom, whirlpool, plus inviting screened-in porch.

► **Seattle Steal.** A hot property in a sizzling market, 3-BR, 2½-BA, 2-story in suburban Bothell has 1,744 sq. ft., fireplace, oak staircase, 2-car garage, big yard. Excellent school district.

► **Phoenix Find.** Ideal '50s ranch in historic district. 2-BR, 2-BA, 1,942 sq. ft. Country kitchen, renovated in '84. Pool, private patio, spacious guest house.

► **New York Nest.** Cozy 780-sq.-ft., 1-BR, 1-BA co-op in pre-WWII Manhattan bldg. on Upper West Side. Private security patrol, plus 24-hr. doorman. Good closets. No AC.

► **D.C. Digs.** A 2-story, 3-BR, 1½-BA Victorian. Transitional NW neighborhood. Updated heating and plumbing, new windows and baths, redone hardwood floors, and remodeled kitchen.

► **Sunshine State.** 4-BR, 2½-BA, 2,000 sq. ft. in planned community of single-family homes 10 mins. west of Boca Raton. Big-deal kitchen, walk-in pantry, laundry, master suite, back porch, pool, and 2-car garage.

► **Ah, Lake Wobegon.** $150K bags sunny 4-yr.-old 3-BR, 2½-BA on 5 acres near desirable Stillwater, 30 mins. east of Mpls. Big kitchen, back porch. Solar heating option plus whirlpool.

► **Bay Area Buy.** On top floor, 1-BR, 1-BA condo in back of bldg. In burgeoning Diamond Heights, overlooking S.F. financial district. 20 mins. from downtown.

► **Hawaii One-Five-Oh.** A real find in the 50th state. 4-BR, 3-BA frame in the hang-loose village of Hauula, 30 miles north of Honolulu. Limited Pacific view—8 miles from North Shore surfing.

► **Mass. Transit.** Snug 4-BR, 2-BA Cape on ¼ acre in Northborough, an hour west of Boston. Easy access to city via Turnpike, Route 9. Skiing nearby. No AC or garage.

4. Locking in the Best Price and Financing

Walter L. Updegrave

Go ahead: choose a house with your heart. But use your sharpest business skills to negotiate the terms of the deal.

Natalie and Kevin Lancaster have come about as close as you can to stealing a house legally. Theirs is a newly built 4-bedroom, 2½-bath, 2,400-square-foot brick contemporary in the fast-growing Bear Creek section of Houston. While similar homes in nearby subdivisions were selling for $125,000 in the fall of 1988, the 32-year-old couple—she's an escrow manager for a title insurer, he's a fleet sales manager for a truck dealership—bought their place for just $84,950. And it gets better. The anxious builder, who told the Lancasters that his construction loan interest was pinching him, also picked up the couple's closing costs of $5,000. Then, to top it off, the builder convinced his lender, Gibraltar Savings, to grant the couple a 30-year fixed-rate mortgage at 9.5 percent—about one percentage point below the going rate at the time. "We're in heaven," says Natalie. "We got a bigger and better house than we ever thought we could afford."

The Lancasters' success story illustrates how shrewd buyers today can pull off spectacular deals on prices and affordable financing, especially in soft real estate markets. In cities such as Baton Rouge, Louisiana, where it would take a year to erase the current inventory of 2,517 house listings, shoppers now have an advantage comparable to holding seven cards in a five-card-stud poker game. So if you're house hunting this year, make sure you capitalize on your superior hand. Otherwise, if you pay too much for a home today, you might be forced to take a loss when you sell one day. "When the housing market was hot, you could count on appreciation to bail you out if you overpaid. That's not true anymore," says W. Bruce Wallin, general manager of PHH Network Services, a relocation company based in Wilton, Connecticut.

As a buyer-borrower, you will have somewhat less leverage with mortgage lenders than with sellers. That's because many banks, savings and loans, mortgage companies, and credit unions have recently stiffened their underwriting policies in response to a U.S. mortgage delinquency rate that hit 6 percent in the mid-'80s versus 4.1 percent in the '70s. As a result, these days you won't find many lenders making 5-percent-down mortgages or no- or low-documentation loans. Nevertheless, lenders are competing furiously for business; one recent bank ad featured a drawing of a loan officer parachuting down to give an airplane passenger a mortgage application. No, bankers won't really go quite that far. Still, in today's competitive mortgage market, there's no need to settle for the first loan dangled before you. By sifting through the traditional menu of fixed- and adjustable-rate mortgages (ARMs), as well as a smorgasbord of newer options like the seven-year balloon and 10-year ARM, you can find a loan tailored to your needs. And should you be relocated by your employer, your company might even pick up some of your financing costs (as more than 40 percent of major corporations now do, according to the Employee Relocation Council).

To squeeze the greatest concessions out of sellers and lenders, you must first gauge the health of the local housing market. The worse it is, the more pressure you can exert. A tip: ask your real estate agent for the average length of time that unsold houses are lingering on the market. If it is 90 days or longer, you are in a buyers' market and can call the shots with sellers and, to a lesser extent, lenders. You should also be realistic about how much house you can afford. As a rule, your housing costs—including insurance and taxes—should not exceed 28 percent of your gross income. This means you can afford a house costing roughly three times your gross.

DEALING WITH THE SELLER

Once you're ready to zero in on specific houses, nose around to determine how anxious the owners are to sell. For example, ask your agent which owners have recently lowered their listing prices by at least 3 percent. "That's often an indication an owner is ripe for a low-ball offer," says William Pivar, author of *Power Real Estate Negotiation* (Longman, $19.95). Never forget, though, that your agent's first allegiance will be to the seller—the person paying him or her the commission. You also stand an excellent chance of negotiating price cuts with sellers who have lived in their houses more than seven years or so. Such owners may be sitting on large enough equity cushions to let them accept a lower price and still post a sizable profit. Furthermore, assuming you have the stomach for it, you could adopt vulture tactics—homing in on owners experiencing financial difficulties. Likely targets: people in mid-divorce, heirs who must raise cash to pay estate taxes, and sellers who, having already bought homes, are stuck making double-barrel mortgage payments each month.

You and the owner can haggle over three financial matters: the sales price, your closing costs—those niggling yet substantial home-buying expenses ranging from title searches to home inspections—and the possibility of seller financing. It's unreasonable to expect to ravage the seller on each, though. Instead, try to bargain on the house price as much as possible. Then, if you think the seller might bend further, press for the other concessions.

Start your negotiations these days by making an aggressive opening bid orally through your agent. This bid should factor in the strength of the local market and the owner's eagerness to sell. Never use the owner's listing price as the basis for your initial offer. Rather, you should peg your bid to the home's market value. To determine this figure, ask your agent for a competitive market analysis showing the prices that comparable houses have sold for within the past six months. Then instruct the agent to draw up a purchase agreement with your offering price, and be sure the contract gives the seller a strict time of three to five days for responding. "As a general rule, your offer should be no higher than the *lowest* price paid for a comparable house in your area during the past six months," says Robert Irwin, author of *Tips and Traps When Buying a Home* (McGraw-Hill,

$12.95). If the local market is depressed and houses typically remain unsold for four months or more, you can try offering 10 percent *below* the past half-year's lowest sales price.

When you're ready to make a prudent bid, don't fall for that favorite harrumphing line of real estate brokers to buyers: "I wouldn't insult my client (the seller) with an offer that low." In fact, this is simply a ploy to get you to raise your offer. If a broker refuses to pass along your bid—and in a soft market anything within 20 percent of the market value should be seriously considered—get yourself another agent.

If you decide to buy a freshly built home, gird yourself for tough bargaining. Builders are often loath to cut sales prices because they know that when the word gets out, prospective buyers of other homes in their subdivisions will demand the same breaks. As the Lancasters discovered, however, builders occasionally get desperate. For example, a builder may be ready to talk when there is a large inventory of new homes in his area—nine months or more. Your local home builders' association may be able to give you such data. Any foreclosed homes for sale in or near a builder's subdivision suggest another chance for dickering since a builder may have to accept less money just to compete. In its Maryland Manor subdivision in Glendale, Arizona, for example, Lennar Homes slashed 17 percent from the price of its townhouses last fall, partly to compete with the U.S. Department of Housing and Urban Development, which was selling 202 repossessed homes in the area.

Typically, a seller will make you a counteroffer in between your bid and the original asking price. It's generally not worth haggling any further if the seller comes back with a figure within 3 percent or so of the price you want. But if you still deem the price too high, let the counter expire. Then make a new bid for an amount between your first offer and the seller's counter. (If you're uncomfortable with negotiating, hire a buyer's broker who will do it for you. Some charge hourly fees of $65 to $100; others keep a percentage of the sales price, usually 3 or 3.5 percent. Call the Real Estate Buyers Agents Council, a national trade group, at 800-359-4092 for names of buyers' brokers near you.)

If you and the seller reach an impasse on price, direct the agent to ask for other concessions that will indirectly lower the house's cost. You can stipulate, for example, that the seller will pick up some or even all of your closing charges, which can easily total 5 percent of the purchase price—$7,500 on a $150,000 home. Try to lay on the seller the points, or loan-processing fees, your lender will charge for your mortgage. One point is equal to 1 percent of the mortgage amount; lenders typically charge buyers one to three points. Of course, if the seller pays your points, you cannot deduct their cost on your tax return (for more tax tips, see "Tax Tips for Buyers," page 44).

Another cost-shaving tactic that's worth considering is asking the seller to lower your mortgage rate for the first few years through what's known as a buy-down, which many lenders offer. This is an especially sound move if you're worried about affording the monthly mortgage payments on the house. Lenders vary their buy-down terms. But in a buy-down on a 10 percent, 30-year fixed-rate $100,000 mortgage, for example, the seller might pay your lender an up-front fee of about $5,100, lowering your interest rate to 7 percent in the loan's first year and cutting the monthly payment from $878 to $665. The rate would then climb one point each year until it locks in at 10 percent in year four.

Mortgage-related costs aren't the only ones you can try to get the seller to pay. Others include a title search (cost: about $200), title insurance ($300 to $600), and appraiser fees ($175 to $300). You'll make any purchase offer contingent upon a home inspection report, naturally (see Chapter 3). If the inspector finds major structural defects or even many minor flaws and you still want the house, have your agent rewrite the contract so that the seller will deduct necessary fix-up costs from your purchase price. In a soft market, you can also demand that the seller pay for—or at least split—the $150 to $300 cost of the inspection itself.

FINDING THE BEST FINANCING

Once you've hammered out the purchase contract for a house, turn your attention to lining up the most suitable financing package. This means not only scouting out the lowest mortgage rate, but also comparing what lenders require for closing costs such as their attorney's fees as well as appraisals and points.

You may be charged between one and four points. But most lenders will let you pay fewer points in exchange for a higher interest rate. For example, instead of owing two points for a 10 percent, 30-year fixed-rate loan, you could pay only one point but your rate would be 10⅛ percent. If you expect to stay in your house for more than five years, you'll probably owe less in overall financing charges by paying more points now and getting the lowest possible mortgage rate.

Don't forget to ask your employer about mortgage assistance. Colgate-Palmolive, for example, pays up to one point in mortgage origination fees for any employee who has been with the company for six months or more. Sometimes, special deals are available in high-priced housing markets. Church & Dwight, the maker of Arm & Hammer baking soda, gives workers at its Princeton, New Jersey, headquarters up to $20,000 toward a down payment and the home buyer doesn't have to repay the money if he stays with the company for five years.

Your first mortgage decision will be whether or not to go for a fixed- or adjustable-rate loan. That choice will hinge on three factors: how much you can afford each month, how you feel about fluctuating payments, and where you think interest rates are headed. A 30-year fixed-rate mortgage (recent rate: 10.25 percent) lets you know in advance exactly what your monthly mortgage payment and interest rate will be for the life of the loan. Adjustable-rate mortgages or ARMs are more affordable initially (recent rate: about 8.4 percent). But their interest rates and monthly payments can rise or fall on specified anniversaries of the loan—usually once a year—depending on the trend of short-term interest rates. While ARM rates may appear low, when they are adjusted, lenders add two to three percentage points, called the margin, to an interest-rate index such as one pegged to Treasuries maturing in one year. Rates on most ARMs, however, cannot be raised by more than two percentage points a year or six points over the life of a mortgage. Still, even if short-term rates haven't budged, the rate on your ARM will go up in the second year.

These days, you are probably better off with a fixed-rate loan. Rates of 10 percent or so are low compared with those during most of the '80s. And you'll get a real bargain with an ARM only if rates drop at least two percentage points over the next few years and then don't head back up. If you think rates will fall but want the option of locking in a rate long term, consider a convertible ARM. After the first year, but before the sixth, you can switch out of the ARM and into a fixed-rate loan, usually for a $250 fee. The new rate will be about one-half of a percentage point more than what lenders are charging at the time for 30-year fixed loans.

Don't be hasty about going with a lender merely because the institution is pushing speedy service or discounts on such goods as appliances and cars. For example, with Citicorp's MortgagePower Plus program, now available in Delaware, New Jersey, New York, and Pennsylvania, a real estate agent takes down such information as your salary and your monthly debt load, and within 15 minutes he or she can give you a commitment on one of six fixed- or adjustable-rate mortgages. You may pay dearly for the speed and convenience of one-stop shopping, however. The real estate agent often gets a fee of one-half of a percentage point of the mortgage amount for making the loan, which raises the cash you will need at closing—by, say, $500 on a $100,000 loan. And by signing up on the spot, you forgo the chance to shop around for a more competitive rate and terms. For example, in northern New Jersey, Citicorp recently charged 10 percent plus three points for a 30-year fixed-rate mortgage, compared with the 9.75-percent-plus-three-point deals at several other local lenders. Moral: "The chances of the first mortgage you look at being the best are virtually nil," warns David Olson, vice president at SMR Research Corporation, a Budd Lake, New Jersey, firm that monitors mortgage-lending trends.

The fastest way to compare local lenders is to scan a current listing of their mortgage rates and terms. Your daily newspaper may publish such a mortgage table. Many real estate brokerage offices also offer guides to mortgages in their areas. Otherwise, order a similar list from one of the companies that conduct weekly surveys. HSH Associates has mortgage data for more than 20 lenders in each of 30 U.S. metropolitan areas (800-873-2837; $18). The *Peeke Report* gives a similar roundup for buyers in Maryland, Virginia, and Washington, D.C. (301-840-5752; $20).

There are now a multitude of mortgages aside from the standard 30-year fixed and one-year Treasury ARM. To help demystify the marketplace, here is a quick rundown of the pros and cons of each:

► **The FHA 30-year fixed-rate loan** (recent rate: 9.5 percent). If you'd like to lock in a low fixed rate on a 30-year loan but can't raise the normal 10 to 20 percent down payment, look into the Federal Housing Administration's mortgage insurance plan offered by many lenders. It permits 3 percent down on the first $25,000 of a home's value, 5 percent for the rest. The catch: the maximum FHA loan amount is generally $67,500, but in high-cost housing markets such as Boston and Los Angeles it's $124,875.

► **The biweekly mortgage** (recent rate: 10.25 percent). Consider this loan if you want the dependability of a fixed-rate deal and want to pay off your loan fast. A biweekly is similar to a standard 30-year fixed-rate mortgage except instead of making, say, an $850 payment each month, you make a $425 payment every two weeks. Since you end up with two extra payments a year, equity builds more quickly and you can pay off the loan in 21 instead of 30 years. (Many lenders will let you transform nearly any mortgage into a biweekly.) Institutions offering biweeklies—as about 25 percent do—may require you to keep your checking account with them so they can automatically withdraw your mortgage payments from the account. So if you don't have a predictable cash flow into your checking account, avoid this arrangement. Otherwise, you could be stuck paying bounced-check fees of $10 to $20 to your lender. And don't bother with a biweekly if you don't have the discipline to make payments every other week.

► **The 15-year fixed-rate loan** (recent rate: 10 percent). If you hate owing anyone anything and want to build up home equity as quickly as possible, this may be the mortgage for you. By cutting the repayment term in half, a borrower with a $150,000 mortgage on a $185,000 house can save $41,000 in total interest payments (at recent rates) compared with a 30-year fixed-rate loan. And after 10 years, he'd have reduced the loan's principal by $74,135 versus only $13,071 on a 30-year fixed or $36,450 on a biweekly. What's more, the interest rate on a 15-year mortgage is usually about a quarter of a percentage point lower than that on a 30-year fixed. So why doesn't everybody take advantage of this great deal? Steep monthly payments—roughly 20 percent higher than those on a 30-year mortgage.

► **Alternative adjustable-rate mortgages** (recent rate range: 8.4 to 10.41 percent). While most ARM lenders offer one-year adjustables tied to Treasury securities, some banks prefer to use other indexes. One common type is the 11th

District cost-of-funds index (COFI), which reflects the interest that West Coast banks generally pay depositors. COFI ARMs are roughly half as volatile as their Treasury counterparts. These deals are common among lenders in California; elsewhere, you may have to make a special request for them.

If you'd like an ARM but the prospect of a new interest rate each year rattles you, search for a lender that offers three- or five-year adjustable loans. These ARMs may give you more protection from higher interest rates—but they also prevent you from benefiting promptly if rates fall. If you don't expect rates to drop much, however, a three- or five-year ARM may provide a lower rate than a 30-year fixed without the roller-coaster moves of a one-year ARM. Should you need a loan for more than $187,450—known as a jumbo—consider a 10-year ARM. Its rate (recently 10.4 percent) remains constant for 10 years and is usually slightly lower than that of a 30-year fixed-rate jumbo (recently 10.7 percent).

► **The seven-year balloon mortgage** (recent rate: 9.75 percent). If you will probably sell the house you are buying within seven years—the average length of home ownership today—this innovative loan, compared with a fixed-rate mortgage, can lower your payments a bit. Here's how the mortgage works: Even though the loan comes due in seven years, monthly payments are kept low because they are calculated as if you had a 30-year mortgage. The rate is set as much as a quarter to a half a percent below that of a conventional 30-year fixed-rate loan, reducing your monthly payments by, say, $40 on a $100,000 loan. When the mortgage comes due in seven years, you can pay it off, or extend its term for 23 years at about a half a point higher than the going rate for 30-year loans, or refinance with another lender. Unlike most ARMs, these balloons have no rate caps, however. Thus if interest rates soar in seven years, so will your monthly costs if you don't pay off the loan.

► **The 30-year graduated-payment mortgage** (recent initial rate: 7.5 percent). This loan is best if you can't afford a home with a conventional fixed or adjustable loan. A graduated-payment mortgage artificially lowers monthly payments during the first five years by basing the payments on a rate that's far below the actual loan rate (recently 10.66 percent). Then the payments rise by about 7.5 percent annually as the borrower's income goes up (or so he or she hopes). After the fifth year, payments remain constant, pegged to the loan's true rate. On a $100,000 graduated-payment loan, for example, monthly payments would now run $705 in the first year and would rise to $1,012 at the start of the sixth year, remaining at that level for the next 24 years. The catch: Since the low initial payments usually don't cover the interest on the loan, the principal balance grows rather than shrinks during the first seven years or so—a feature known in banking circles as negative amortization. So if you want to sell your house during that period and its price hasn't risen, your sale proceeds may not cover your mortgage balance and any broker's commission. You'd then have to tap into your savings to pay off the mortgage—exactly the opposite of what you probably expect when you first buy a home.

HOW TO BUY HOMEOWNERS INSURANCE

Before you can move into a house, your lender will require you to buy homeowners insurance. Don't shrug off this expense—typically $300 to $600 a year on a $100,000 house—as another forgettable closing cost. As the victims of Hurricane Hugo and the Bay Area earthquake learned, adequate coverage can mean the difference between ruin and recovery after a disaster. This guide will help you buy wisely.

What's covered. The best policies adequately protect your house, its contents, and you—the last against lawsuits if someone is injured on your property, or say, sues you when your lovable pooch wanders down the street and takes a chunk out of a stroller's calf. Buy the broadest coverage you can afford. Be aware, though, that policies usually cover a home for only 80 percent of its replacement value—what it would cost you to rebuild. Insurance against flood and earthquake damage is never part of the standard package. Home buyers in flood-prone areas should ask their agents for coverage from the National Flood Insurance Program, a federal plan that costs about $200 to $300 a year for a $150,000 house. To get quake coverage, you typically must buy what's known as an endorsement; some companies sell the insurance as a separate policy. The price depends on where you live; in California you might pay $300 to $600 a year for a $200,000 house.

Most policies automatically insure your belongings like furniture and clothing for half the coverage you carry on your house. If 50 percent seems low—for example, if you are a home electronics fiend—pay for more protection. Contents coverage of 70 percent might raise your annual premiums by 10 to 15 percent. Certain valuables have their own coverage limits. For instance, theft losses on jewelry and furs are generally insured only up to $1,000; silverware, $2,500. For extra protection, you'll pay from 40¢ per $100 of additional silverware insurance to $4 per $100 for jewelry.

Almost all policies automatically provide $100,000 of personal-liability insurance for you and your household. It's cheap to raise that protection, and in today's litigious society it's probably wise. For another $5 to $15 a year, you can get $300,000 of coverage. You might need even more, though, if you are a tempting target such as a highly paid executive. If so, ask your agent about an umbrella policy—excess liability insurance that comes in $1 million increments above your homeowners and auto insurance protection. Cost: about $150 a year for $1 million in coverage. Homeowners policies also generally pay additional living expenses—up to 10 percent of your home's coverage—if you must evacuate during rebuilding.

Crucial clauses. Tell your agent you want a guaranteed-replacement-value clause that requires the insurer to pay the full cost to repair or rebuild your home. Otherwise, you'll get reimbursed only up to the policy's limit. Also, get replacement-cost coverage for your belongings so you won't be docked for their depreciation. Expect to pay 10 to 15 percent extra for each clause.

Discounts to demand. Most policies come with a $250 deductible—the amount you must pay per loss before the insurer provides benefits. By raising the deductible to $500, you can shave 5 to 10 percent off your premiums. Many insurers also offer discounts of 10 percent if your home has a fire or security alarm that rings at a nearby fire or police station.

—*Teresa Tritch*

A GUIDE TO MORTGAGE CHOICES

Lenders now offer so many types of mortgages that the selective home buyer can easily find one to match his wallet and taste. Here are the most common varieties, their recent interest rates, and brief guidelines for choosing a deal that is perfectly tailored to your needs.

		On a loan of $100,000		
Mortgage type	Recent interest rate	Initial monthly payment	Annual income needed to qualify	Best for
30-year fixed rate	10.25%	$ 896	$43,000	Buyers who demand stable payments; deals are most appealing when rates drop below 10%
Fixed-rate biweekly	10.25	448 (biweekly)	43,000	Paying off your loan faster without owing higher monthly payments
15-year fixed rate	10.00	1,075	51,600	Quickly building home equity—if you can afford the high monthly payment
Seven-year balloon	9.75	863	41,400	Buyers who expect to move or refinance within seven years, paying off the loan
One-year adjustable (Treasury index)	8.44	773	37,100	Borrowers who need a low initial rate to qualify for a home or ones who think rates will soon fall
One-year adjustable (cost-of-funds index)	8.40	765	36,700	Getting a low initial rate plus rates in later years that won't fluctuate as much as those on Treasury adjustables
10-year adjustable	10.41	905	43,400	Beating the rate on a 30-year fixed-rate jumbo loan without the volatility of a 1-year adjustable
30-year graduated payment	10.66*	705	33,800	Borrowers who need a low initial rate to qualify for a home but can afford payment increases that kick in after the first year

*Actual loan rate; monthly payment and income needed to qualify are based on the first-year rate of 7.5 percent.

TAX TIPS FOR BUYERS

Financing your home means learning how to work with your silent partner, the Internal Revenue Service. To assist you, here's a short course in the tax fundamentals of buying a house (tax advice for homeowners, remodelers, and sellers appears on pp. 55, 71, and 82).

Your basic home-purchase expenses, as well as recurring costs, are fully or partly deductible on Schedule A. The allowable write-offs:

Mortgage interest. The rules to qualify for this deduction are straightforward. The home must be your primary residence or a second residence that is for your personal use; the total mortgage debt to buy your homes must not exceed $1 million; and the loan must be secured by the house.

Your share of property taxes and mortgage interest you pay in escrow. The IRS lets you and the seller prorate the taxes and interest for the year you buy. But you cannot deduct the seller's shares, even if you pay them.

Points. You can deduct all mortgage points—sometimes called loan-origination fees—on a principal residence if your points are comparable to what local institutions commonly demand. The points must also represent an interest charge, not a fee for bank services. Make sure that you pay the points by check. Some lenders simply subtract the charge from your mortgage amount and lend you the balance. That may be a convenience—but it will cost you the deduction.

Moving expenses. If you buy a house in a work-related move, you may be able to write off a truckload of expenses. There are two catches: your new job must be at least 35 miles farther from your previous home than your old job was from that residence, and you must work at the new job for 39 weeks in the 12 months after the move (78 weeks in 24 months if you are self-employed). Pass those tests and you can fully deduct house-hunting trips and the cost of shipping your household goods. You will also be able to claim as much as $3,000 in other moving expenses, such as temporary living cost incurred while house hunting. To claim moving expenses, file a 1040 and a special form, 3903.

As with all tax breaks, proper documentation is critical.

Even records of nondeductible closing costs such as a lawyer's fee, title insurance, and real estate transfer taxes can be valuable tax savers. That's because when you sell your house and determine its basis (taxspeak for value), you can add those costs to your purchase price and thus lower the taxes you will eventually owe on your gain. "If you set up a file once you decide to buy a home, you'll be off to a tax-smart start," says Martin Shenkman, a tax attorney in New York City and author of *The Total Real Estate Tax Planner* (John Wiley & Sons, $12.95).

—*T.T.*

5. The Rooms You Will View

Joanna L. Krotz

Anything old may be fashionable now, but, reports Lois Thibault, who heads up Vision 2000, a research program of the American Institute of Architects, "the trend toward nostalgia in design really means turn-of-the-century vocabulary wrapped around high-tech choices." That elegant old place down the street with 19th-century moldings now sports a double-glazed, energy-efficient skylight letting in the sunshine. All around the house, upstairs and downstairs, rooms are being rethought and customized to suit contemporary needs, solve two-career space problems, and, in general, soothe our souls.

Kitchens, for instance, have gone user-friendly. So no longer is one lone ranger (read: the woman of the house) banished to solitary showdowns with the stove. Instead, the cooking area has opened into a warm entertaining and dining room that welcomes the whole family—sometimes with a walk-in pantry and even a corner home office. Upstairs or nestled into a wing, you now find luxuriously appointed master bedroom suites that take the edges off stress-filled days. Children's rooms are thoughtfully designed for real-kid needs with, for instance, tables that grow up into desks. And somewhere in the house, you'll see more examples of personally designed space—a woodworking studio, library, home gym, or landscaped yards and gardens that are like outdoor rooms. When we checked in with the producers of *thirtysomething* about the babyboom blueprint for the home, we found just these '90s priorities for our TV pals, the Steadmans of Philadelphia. "Now that Michael's got more income," explains the show's production designer, Brandy

Alexander, "he and Hope will be fixing up the house, expanding the kitchen, remodeling the sunroom, and perhaps screening in the porch to bring in the outdoors." And of course, she says, "Hope and Michael will have the same problems with contractors that we all do."

THE BIG FAMILY KITCHEN

First, pull down the walls between kitchen and dining room, letting in light, space, mood, and, most of all, friends and co-cooks. Next, install some plumped-up, plunk-yourself-down seating for the gang. Add a sleek work island, some stools, perhaps a mantel and hearth, and there you have it—the most important room in the house.

THE MASTER SUITE

Today's bigger and better master suite takes the strain out of extra laps around the fast track. It should feel like a tucked-away living room for two, with such amenities as a sitting area, home electronics, perhaps a fridge, exercise bike, or fireplace. Close by is the extended, elegant bath, with whirlpool or soaking tub, two-career sinks, and dressing rooms. Welcome home, indeed.

PERSONAL PRIORITIES

At the top of any '90s agenda is investing time and money to create a home so personalized that you never want to leave. "The house is becoming a vacation spot," says William Devereaux of Berkus Group Architects. Character—both yours and the house's—counts. A fitness buff might convert her spare room into a StairMaster to the stars. The weekend gardener bumps out a back wall for a greenhouse. Helped by their designers and architects, the nation's semipro potters, painters, and photographers are busy putting their stamp on personal space.

6. When It's Better to Remodel Than Move

Walter L. Updegrave

You can often get the house you want without moving. But renovate because you love the place, not because you figure to profit on the deal.

If you own a house, you've undoubtedly also daydreamed about living in the perfect one: with spacious sun-filled rooms, a regal bath, a country kitchen chockablock with cabinets and counter space, and a private retreat for getting away from it all. During those musings, you probably assumed that this ideal house was out there somewhere—maybe even under construction right now—if only you could find and afford it. Actually, you may already be living in it, though it may not seem so. "Millions of people feel they are misfits in their own homes," says Duo Dickinson, a Madison, Connecticut, architect who specializes in renovation. "The lifestyle of the 1990s simply doesn't jibe with the lifestyle that most houses were built for." Fortunately, a renovation that redesigns the existing space within your house—or creates additional rooms where necessary—can custom-tailor your home precisely to the way you live.

These days, renovating and redecorating have become hotter than dancing the *lambada*. According to the National Association of Home Builders (NAHB), homeowners will pay $103 billion to improve their residences in 1990, more than double the tab of only seven years ago and roughly two-thirds of what Americans will spend this year to *buy* new houses. Even George and Barbara Bush will be getting into the act. The nation's First Occupants, who have no plans to trade up anytime soon, just asked Congress for $500,000 to renovate the White House's 25-foot-by-25-foot main kitchen and two smaller ones for the 20 or so functions they throw each month.

Millions of other Americans have discovered that improving often beats moving in today's ho-hum housing markets. With home prices nationally projected to rise at roughly 5 percent a year, it may take three or more years of appreciation to recoup the transaction costs of buying, selling, and moving. Result: to get the house you want, you're sometimes better off staying put and fixing up. Then too, many owners of period-style homes get a charge out of restoring their residences. "Renovating a Victorian is a way of connecting with older values," says Wendy Jordan, editor of *Remodeling* magazine. There can be powerful emotional attachments to staying put too, especially for families. "The kids are often settled in school, and the parents have a network they can rely on, from friends to relatives to babysitters," says Walter Stoeppelwerth, publisher of HomeTech Publications in Bethesda, Maryland. "It's hard to rip all that up just for a bigger house somewhere else."

Remodeling can also solve problems encountered when you outgrow your house, as Jeremy Starobin, 38, and his wife Debby Derman, 37, found three years ago. At the time, the couple—he owns a company that installs skylights and greenhouses, she's a homemaker—owned a $165,000 ranch-style home on about an acre in Blue Bell, Pennsylvania, an affluent Philadelphia suburb. But the tiny, 1,100-square-foot place had only two small bedrooms, and Debby was pregnant with Benjamin. Rather than sell and relocate, they doubled their space by building a two-story addition. It has an 18-foot-by-22-foot master bedroom and luxurious dual-vanity bath with a whirlpool tub plus two extra bedrooms that are now used as an office and a guest room. Two-year-old Benjamin and the couple's latest addition, five-month-old Jonathan, live in the two small bedrooms in the older part of the house. The family didn't move out during the four-month, $80,000 project. But unlike others for whom renovation has proved daily torture, the household suffered minimum inconvenience because a plastic tarp separated them from the construction. "In remodeling, we definitely made the right decision," Jeremy says. "We wound up with a house that fits our needs perfectly."

If you too might want to undertake a big improvement project, it's essential to find ways to keep your costs down and your potential payback up. For starters, don't try to justify a splashy renovation by claiming it will make a great investment. In a 1989 NAHB survey of 1,600 people who remodeled their homes, respondents estimated that on average they added 95¢ of value for every dollar they spent. Actually, unless you are starting with a house whose value is well below that of others in the area, you will probably be lucky to get back anything near that much when you sell. More often than not, as is the case with such jobs as building a 12-foot-by-16-foot sunroom addition, you may get back just 60 percent or so of your investment. Keep in mind, too, that remodeling costs vary by region. For example, a recent *Remodeling* magazine survey estimates it now costs roughly $36,500 to build a 400-square-foot family room addition in pricey Los Angeles, compared with only $25,000 in Columbia, South Carolina. (For average costs and paybacks of popular projects, see the table on p. 57.) Says Bryan Patchan, executive director of the NAHB Remodelers Council: "You should remodel to make your house more comfortable and enjoyable—not just to make it a better investment."

For some owners, merely spending a few thousand dollars on home furnishing touches can customize a house for much less than an expensive structural overhaul. No longer must you feel constrained to decorate all at once in a single and often expensive motif, though. Rather, today's more adventurous owners now gradually fill their homes through a sophisticated mix: perhaps a $2,000 French country-style armoire here, a hand-painted $395 Italian *faux* marble table there. "This eclecticism not only makes your house a medium of self-expression," says Judy George, chairman and chief executive officer of Domain, a chain of 10 home furnishing stores based in Norwood, Massachusetts; "it adds a sense of romance and color that makes living in the house exciting and fun."

Should you decide, however, that the way to make your house most livable is through a major renovation, you can help prevent the project from turning into a financial folly by adhering to two simple rules. The first is what the NAHB's Bryan Patchan calls the 20 percent rule: don't undertake any project that will raise the value of your home to more than 20 percent above the most expensive houses in the neighborhood. Spend more on the job, and you'll have trouble getting your money back when you sell.

Rule 2 is to remodel when the housing market in your area is in a slump. During a frenzied market, competition between builders and remodelers for contractors and supplies bids up both materials and labor costs. In addition, remodelers feel more confident about charging higher prices when customers are lining up at their doors. Your remodeling costs can be 10 to 20 percent lower when the housing market is slow in your area.

One of the best ways to add space is by transforming your attic into a more functional room. This is a particularly useful technique in tight urban settings and neighborhoods where small lots preclude adding on. Though normally shunned as a dark, cramped, dusty area with inadequate head room, an attic can actually be converted into an open, bright home office or an extra bedroom with bath when renovated by a skilled architect or contractor. Typical cost: about $15,000 to $25,000, roughly $1,200 to $2,400 more with skylights.

The flip side of the house—the basement—is another area that lends itself to carving out room. For roughly $25,000 to $35,000, you could turn an unfinished 24-foot-by-40-foot basement into either a recreation room plus bath or two extra bedrooms and a bath. But don't expect to recoup more than 50 percent or so of what you spend. "It's hard to get enough light into most basements," says Stoeppelwerth. "As a result, home buyers don't value extra living space there very highly these days."

Since kitchens and bathrooms are prone to show their age, many homeowners launch their renovations in these areas. In addition to bringing your home into the '90s, renovating these rooms can make it easier to unload your house at resale time. The demand for a modern, fully equipped kitchen is so powerful among home shoppers, for example, that you can usually count on recouping a higher percentage of what you spend on a renovation there than with any other project—88 percent on average. You will get a more modest payback when remodeling an existing bathroom—about 73 percent on average—but adding a second full bath to a house that has only one can boost your payback to 85 percent.

Many couples with children now choose to add privacy and luxury by putting in master suites with bed, bath, and separate areas large enough for, say, a small gym or a study. The most cost-efficient way to achieve this effect is by combining two bedrooms. Expect to pay $15,000—roughly $45 a square foot. But toss in splurges such as enlarging the existing bath to include a whirlpool tub and walk-in shower, and the price tag can easily float above $20,000 to $25,000. Though adding a master suite can let you recoup 79 percent of your money, real estate brokers caution against this project if you won't have at least three bedrooms left after eliminating one. Reason: a two-bedroom house is a hard sell in most communities.

If you're already using your square footage to the maximum but your family still feels claustrophobic, look into a room addition. The cost will depend on the size of the addition and the materials you use, but figure on paying roughly $70 to $100 per square foot. To increase its payback potential, design the addition to compensate for any weaknesses in the house's present layout. If your home has a tiny kitchen segregated from the family room, for example, an addition that creates a family room opening onto the kitchen will add the most resale value.

As land costs rise and houses get shoehorned onto smaller lots in many densely populated areas, homeowners are also looking for novel ways to get the most from the outdoor space they have, often by creating what some design mavens call an outdoor room. A patio or deck, for example, offers the chance of getting extra functional space at a low cost, particularly if you build it off the kitchen, family room, or dining room, where it can be used for alfresco entertaining. You might pay only $4,400 to $5,600 for a 16-foot-by-20-foot deck made of pressure-treated pine; 25 to 50 percent more for more durable redwood or cedar. A deck doesn't usually add much to resale value, although you stand a better chance of getting a decent payback if the deck looks onto a mountain, lake, or ocean.

Another way to elevate the satisfaction you get from your outdoor space, if not your home's value, is to use trees and shrubs for decoration and privacy. For instance, by spending as little as $2,500 to plant dogwoods, Japanese maples, and shrubs like yews and azaleas, you can fashion an outdoor sanctuary. With leisure time at a premium, however, you'll probably want to scout out low-maintenance landscaping techniques. One way to make caring for your property easier is to use bark chips or pachysandra as ground cover. Then too, even though horticultural scientists haven't yet come up with no-mow lawns, an improved breed of grass known as fescues—sold at garden centers in 50-pound seed bags at about $90 each—requires far less watering and fertilizing than more common varieties. So instead of spending time taking care of your property, you can relax and watch it take care of itself.

FIVE SMART HOME-CONTROL SYSTEMS

The trouble with some homes is that they don't think for their owners. You can get your residence to wise up, though. Just purchase an electronic system that lets you program it to maintain your place exactly as you wish. Cost: anywhere from $20 for a simple programmable thermostat that regulates temperature to upwards of $100,000 for the latest all-in-one units that combine high-tech security alarms with systems that let you phone home to turn on the lights and start the microwave.

Before you go for the most Jetson-like of the technologies, realize that many of the products now on the market are little more than gimmicks. So when you see a fascinating unit, the most elaborate of which are typically sold by home-security companies, ask yourself these questions: Does it make my life easier—such as a security- or heating-control system? Does it enhance my life—such as allowing my VCR and television to communicate? And finally, does it cost too much? Tricia Parks, a home automation consultant in Dallas, notes that if reducing utility costs is your primary objective, you should also inquire about how much the product has cut fuel bills in houses like yours.

When comparing systems, decide which kinds of controls seem most comfortable to you. The choices run from modules plugged into outlets to infrared remote controls, Touch-Tone phones, touch screens, and voice-activated systems. Generally, the jazzier the type, the snazzier the price.

A complete rundown on hundreds of products appears in the latest *Buying Guide* from *Electronic House* magazine (56790 Magnetic Drive, Mishawaka, Indiana 46545; $5).

What follow, however, are five gadgets that technology consultants say are worth considering. They are listed from the least to the most expensive. You can buy the first two in hardware stores or home centers and hook them up yourself. The others require a call to the companies mentioned for the name of a local firm that can show you the product and install it; prices include typical installation costs.

The X-10 Powerhouse Control System. You plug your lights and appliances into X-10 timer modules that hook into outlets. Then you can program the works to go on or off at preset times with a controller. The X-10 costs about $13 per module and up to $50 for each controller. Says Roger Dooley, publisher of *Electronic House:* "If your only concern is having the coffee ready at the same time each morning or the driveway lights turned on at night, this is a fairly complete system."

Honeywell's Call-in Control. As the name suggests, Call-in Control ($50) lets you operate lights or appliances by telephone. So, for example, you can phone home from work to turn on a window air conditioner a few hours before you arrive home.

Teletimer Energy Saving Service, or TESS (407-994-9044). This is a joint test project, now available only in south Florida and the Washington, D.C., area, from Bell Atlantic and Teletimer, a home automation firm. If you pay about $100 to install a device that resembles a thermostat plus $12 a month thereafter, it will link household systems like heating, cooling, and sprinklers to a phone company computer that regulates them. Tell TESS to turn on your sprinklers at 5 P.M. and it will do it—unless it has rained, in which case the computer overrides the command.

Unity Systems' Home Manager (415-369-3233). Think of Home Manager, a $6,000 to $15,000 combination security system and regulator of appliances and utilities, as the ultimate room tutor. A 14-inch-diagonal touch screen showing a floor plan of your home is built into a wall and wired into each room. You can then, for example, set the porch light to go off in the morning at the same time your living room light flicks on. The security setup can be particularly useful when you're away but others are home. You can rig it to go off if, say, contractors working in the kitchen venture upstairs. The room where the offense has occurred will also flash on your screen.

Custom Command System (301-454-7158). Considered the Rolls-Royce of home automation, this all-in-one package costs between $40,000 and $100,000. For that price, you can buy a wall box that programs a security alarm, lights, heating, TVs, and VCRs, as well as stereos and CD players, by any of the five methods of operation. One soothing option: the system can be outfitted with snow sensors atop your roof that automatically switch on Custom Command's underground driveway heaters, to melt the snow and eliminate shoveling.

—Debra Wishik Englander

TAX TIPS FOR OWNERS

The first tax rule of home ownership is: be a pack rat. Records of improvements such as bills, blueprints, and canceled checks become vital tax documents because the expenses will reduce your capital-gains taxes, if any, when you sell.

To qualify as an improvement, the work must add value to your house or prolong its usefulness. Examples: converting an attic into living space, installing central air conditioning, and adding a bathroom. Basic repairs and maintenance like the cost of painting or fixing broken windows generally have no tax value. Some tax advisers, however, consider extensive repairs such as refinishing hardwood floors or replastering walls to be tax-cutting improvements. If you want to test this gray area of the law, be sure you have before and after photos to show the IRS in case you're audited.

Aside from mortgage interest and property taxes, a few other homeowning expenses are deductible, usually on Schedule A of Form 1040:

Assessment charges. You can write off interest and maintenance charges on special property assessments such as those for new roads, sidewalks, and sewer lines. But you can't deduct the assessments themselves.

Casualty losses. If you experience a sudden, unexpected and unusual loss, you can write off any unreimbursed costs that exceed 10 percent of your adjusted gross income plus $100. Losses from thefts and natural disasters qualify for the deduction; those from termites don't.

Home offices. The cost of maintaining a home office is

deductible if you use it regularly and exclusively for business. If you're an employee, the office must be for the boss's—not your own—convenience. Deductible costs include a pro rata share of mortgage interest, utilities, homeowners insurance, repairs, and depreciation. Your annual write-off is limited to your net income from the office.

Medical expenses. You may be able to claim the cost of permanent home improvements prescribed by a doctor. Examples: an air-purifying system for allergies, an elevator for severe arthritis, or a swimming pool for a chronic back problem. When calculating the write-off, you must include only the portion of the expense that does not add to your home's value. You can claim such unreimbursed expenses only to the extent that they exceed 7.5 percent of your adjusted gross income.

Second homes. Mortgage interest and taxes are fully deductible when the house is purely for your personal use. Ditto if you rent out the place but use it yourself at least 14 days a year or 10 percent of the time it's rented, whichever is greater. Rent the house longer, however, and you become subject to more complicated rules that warrant a trip to your tax adviser's office.

—Teresa Tritch

REMODELING PAYBACKS

As the following table of U.S. averages shows, you are unlikely to recoup 100 percent of your investment on these common renovation jobs, listed from the greatest payback potential of 88 percent to the lowest. A kitchen remodeling tends to hold the most value, since the room is usually a major draw for buyers. Doing a job yourself can save you as much as two-thirds of the cost of hiring a contractor, but you should factor in the value of your time to calculate your true savings.

Project	Cost if done by a contractor	Materials only	Cost recouped at resale	Comments
Renovate the kitchen	$20,641	$7,224	88%	Adds more value than most remodeling projects and can really help to sell a house; go for high-quality cabinetry; don't stint on storage and counter space
Add a bathroom	10,151	2,538	85	The 85% payback presumes you are adding a second full bath to a house with just one; returns drop sharply when you add more than two baths
Convert the master bedroom into a suite with bath	21,074	4,847	79	Combining two bedrooms to form a private retreat has become a popular project; makes an older house competitive with newer homes at resale
Build a family room	31,223	7,494	78	Do this off the kitchen to create an open gathering area sought by new-home buyers; resale value drops if the addition's style clashes with the rest of the house
Put on a family room with fireplace	35,169	8,402	76	A family room hearth adds comfort and coziness to a new addition, and many buyers are big on fireplaces
Remodel a bathroom	7,568	2,422	73	A useful project in houses 25 or more years old; hedonistic splurges like a marble tub and vanities can easily push costs to $30,000
Construct a deck	5,109	2,146	67	An inexpensive way to add usable space to the house, though the payback is relatively low; returns are slightly higher for decks with scenic views

Source: *Remodeling* magazine, © 1989 Hanley-Wood, Inc.; materials costs by HomeTech Remodeling and Renovation Cost Estimator.

7. How to Survive a Home Improvement

Clint Willis

The remodeling process is rarely heavenly, but there are steps you can take to prevent it from turning into a living hell.

Actor Don Johnson was the perfect expression of mid-'80s cool when he played detective Sonny Crockett on *Miami Vice*. But in real life, Johnson can get hot. Just ask him about building contractors. Back in late 1988, when he and actress Melanie Griffith, now his wife, tried to renovate the $1 million, 15-room 1930s farmhouse that they share near Aspen, Colorado, a local construction outfit gave them fits. Apparently the feeling was mutual. Seven months and $508,272 into the job, Johnson fired the firm. Among his gripes: gaps in the pine floors, sagging ceiling beams, and a leaky whirlpool bathtub. For its part, the contractor countered by saying that its workers fixed some of the problems, that others were structural ones the firm wasn't asked to correct, and that Johnson himself told the contractors to give the floors a rustic look. The contractors filed for arbitration, demanding $95,813 in unpaid bills for themselves and subcontractors. Said Johnson in a press statement: "Anyone who has ever been on the receiving end of an incompetent contractor should be able to understand my frustration and anger."

Don and Melanie are hardly ordinary homeowners, but their remodeling experience is all too typical. Some 8,200 owners complained to Better Business Bureaus about their home remodeling contractors in 1988; only nine of the 137 types of companies tracked by the BBB generated more gripes. Clearly, fixing up is hard to do. What can go wrong? What *can't?* In Pentagonian fashion, major home renovations costing $10,000 and up are legend for their cost overruns, missed deadlines, and shoddy workmanship. Add to that several months of dust, disorder, and din, and—well, you get the idea. The truth is, it's almost impossible to hire someone to create a master suite, remodel a kitchen, or convert a basement into a playroom without disruptions or screwups. But there are numerous ways of preventing or at least minimizing the financial and construction snafus that so often bedevil renovations. The three keys: choosing reliable professionals, hammering out detailed contracts with them, and holding them to the agreements.

First, though, decide precisely how and what you want to remodel or renovate. San Diego attorneys Lesa Wilson, 32, and husband Scott Loosen, 35, credit the success of their $145,000 renovation to the four years they spent considering ideas for reshaping their 1,000-square-foot $280,000 home near the beach and almost tripling its size. They rejected no fewer than 10 designs before settling on the one that best met their primary goal: getting their kitchen to open onto their backyard for easier outdoor entertaining. The couple ultimately chose an architect who designed and helped monitor the job. Among the tasks: transforming their garage into a kitchen, turning the old kitchen into a guest bedroom, and converting the first-floor bedroom into a 220-square-foot dining room. The entire project took seven-and-a-half months and came in within $10,000 of their original budget. "If we had remodeled without seeing all the designs," says Lesa, "we wouldn't have been as happy with the results."

A critical pre-remodeling step is honestly appraising whether you have the temperament to put up with the aggravation of a renovation. If your remodeling job will consume more than 50 percent of your home's living space or key rooms such as your kitchen or the only full bathroom, you will probably need to camp elsewhere until the work is done. For smaller projects, plan on getting to know your remodelers *very* well; just ask TV's Murphy Brown about Eldin, her ubiquitous house painter.

FINDING THE HELP YOU NEED

Start any renovation by asking yourself whether you can handle alone small fix-up projects like installing light fixtures or floor tiles. Some excellent how-to books, such as the *Reader's Digest Complete Do-It-Yourself Manual* ($22.95) and the *Home Repair and Improvement* series ($10.99 per book; published by Time-Life Books, a subsidiary of the *Money Guide's* parent company) may be all you'll need. (For more advice about do-it-yourself projects, see page 64.) No matter how handy you are, you will need professional help for big jobs. Relatively straightforward improvements—a new kitchen, say, or a room addition that doesn't change the structure of your home—can most easily be handled by a contractor who does both design work and construction. Such contractors often call their companies design/build firms. The contractor will then subcontract carpenters, plumbers, and other workers, buy materials, organize work schedules, and follow the job's day-to-day progress.

If you plan something that will dramatically change the design of your home, such as replacing two bedrooms with a master suite or opening up a kitchen to include a family area, you will probably get the best results by hiring two types of experts: first, either an architect or an interior designer to plan and oversee the project, and then a contractor to build it. Architects are best for jobs involving structural changes such as moving walls. Interior designers generally specialize in making existing rooms more livable. For instance, they can devise a more appropriate lighting system and order hard-to-find furniture, wallpaper, and other accessories. You'll pay an architect or designer a fee of roughly 10 to 15 percent of anticipated construction costs, or $10,000 to $15,000 on a $100,000 remodeling job.

Your Yellow Pages probably lists dozens of contractors, architects, and interior designers, so selecting ones to improve your home can be a daunting task. Neighbors or acquaintances who have had work done similar to the renovation you plan can refer you to likely candidates. Beyond that, here's how to narrow your search:

► **Start by writing to professional organizations for names and phone numbers of architects or interior designers in your area.** The local chapter of the American Institute of Architects can refer you to registered architects who have passed state licensing examinations. Similarly, the local chapter of the American Society of Interior Designers will provide information on its members who have graduated from a four- or five-year degree program.

► **Set up appointments with at least three architects or designers to explain what you want, why you're remodeling, and how you expect the changes to mesh with your lifestyle.** Most will meet with you for an hour or so at no charge to discuss your ideas. Before you hire an architect, be sure he or she has handled projects similar in scale to yours; many specialize instead in new construction.

► **Investigate contractors by asking local architects and designers for referrals.** In addition, call your local builders' association for names of contractors who are among the National Association of Home Builders' 130 certified graduate remodelers. These people have at least five years of experience owning or managing a remodeling company and take continuing-education courses. Interview at least three contractors and ask them for your project. Don't jump at the smallest fee. "The guy with the low bid may take his profit out of the job by using shoddy materials or taking shortcuts," maintains Frank Spivey Jr., president of Spivey Construction, a respected design/build firm in Indianapolis.

When you've identified a promising contractor, find out the answers to these three questions:

► **Is he solvent?** "The biggest disaster is watching your contractor go out of business in the middle of a job," says Todd A. Russell, president of T.A. Russell Construction in Glendora, California. In addition to the delay, expense, and inconvenience of finding someone to finish the project, you may face claims from subcontractors who have not been paid for their work on the job. For a clue to a contractor's financial stability, ask for names and phone numbers of his regular subcontractors and suppliers. Then call them to see whether he typically pays promptly. If he has been slow lately, that may be a signal of money trouble. Also, be wary of newcomers; an estimated 90 percent of new contractors go out of business within five years.

► **Is he reliable?** Contractors rarely say no to a job. You'll get your best gauge of reliability by visiting at least one of the contractor's clients who recently lived through a remodeling project like yours. Any reputable contractor will gladly provide such references. Find out how well the contractor met his deadlines and estimated his fee. Since problems probably arose during the renovation—they nearly always do—ask whether the contractor handled them satisfactorily. Inquire too whether the work and materials matched the standards originally agreed upon by the owner and contractor. In addition, be sure the contractor will be using his regular team for your job, not the second-string pickups he might use when he's juggling a number of projects. If he tells you the staff he'll assign has worked with him for less than six months and most of the subcontractors have never worked for him, find another contractor.

► **Is he honest?** The Better Business Bureau can tell you if any complaints have been filed against a contractor. You might also check his probity by getting in touch with local suppliers and architects.

GETTING THE CONTRACT RIGHT

A contract from an architect or interior designer, usually a one-to eight-page document, spells out fees and payment terms as well as a general description of the work the pro will do. For example, the contract might say that your architect will offer three alternative detailed designs and will visit the job site at least once a week. Ask your lawyer to review the contract.

You need to bear down especially hard on a contractor's contract because of its minutia. Every aspect of the renovation should be included. Even a modest job—renovating a small kitchen, for example—might call for two to three pages of specifications, known in the trade as specs. Show this contract to your lawyer, and to your architect or designer if you're using one. For $5.95, the American Homeowners Foundation, a private group, will provide an eight-page model agreement that you can compare with yours (1724 S. Quincy Street, Arlington, Virginia 22204). If anything is missing from your contract, such as deadlines, brand names, or descriptions of materials, write it in before signing.

Be certain that your agreement also lays out the following information:

► **The price calculation and your payment schedule.** There are two types of contracts: fixed-price and time-and-materials. A fixed-price contract guarantees your costs. If anything comes up during the job that will change the project, you and the contractor must then sign an official change order noting—and agreeing to—any additional related expenditures. In a time-and-materials contract, you will get only a rough estimate of the renovation's cost. Your actual fee will depend on the hours of labor and expenses ultimately incurred. A fixed-price contract is safer, since you lock in costs early.

With either type, stipulate the payment schedule. On a fixed-price contract, never pay more than 30 percent of the anticipated cost when you sign the contract. The rest should break down roughly this way: 30 percent midway through the job, 30 percent when the major work is done, and 10 percent after all remaining details are complete. Make payments for a time-and-materials contract every two weeks or so to cover ongoing costs.

► **The precise materials.** Will you get prebuilt, modular cabinets (cost: $50 to $60 a foot) or custom-made cherry ones (cost: $125 a foot)? Other key concerns: the thickness and exterior finish of new walls; ceiling textures; brand names and styles of windows, doors, plumbing fixtures, and appliances; and the number of electrical plugs, lights, and switches in a room. Material names and descriptions won't always be familiar, so ask for catalog pictures or visit showrooms if necessary.

LIMITING UNPLEASANT SURPRISES

Even if you hire an architect or a designer to supervise the project, it's essential to be on the lookout for missteps along the way. Check on materials as they arrive to be sure you're getting what you were promised. If you must move out of the house during the job, visit unannounced several times a week to make sure that work is progressing according to your schedule and design.

Be firm but reasonable when your contractor misses a deadline. Occasional slippage is to be expected, particularly when there's a reasonable cause. Examples: a snowstorm delays roofwork or the building-supply store must special-order the faucets you crave.

If your home is old or has an unusual design, expect other surprises as well. In 1988, Portland, Oregon, real estate broker Dale Bernards, 32, and his wife Karen, 29, a dental hygienist, renovated their unusual residence: an imposing 6,000-square-foot castle modeled after one in Canterbury, England. When the Bernards hired an architect and contractor to enlarge and brighten their kitchen, they were told the job would cost $26,000 and take only two months. But an 11-foot arch on a curved kitchen wall ended up needing nine coats of plaster. Resetting the decorative windows to make them open and close required unanticipated extensive drilling. Result: the job took three-and-a-half months and ended up $3,000 over budget, an expense the couple decided *they* had to pay because they felt the architect and contractor weren't responsible for such unforeseen problems. The passage of time lets the Bernards laugh off their experience now. "With an old house, you have to expect everything," says Karen.

When your renovation is finally over but before you've made that last payment, review the work with your contractor to see that all the specs were met. Test the toilets, sinks, and tubs for plumbing leaks; look for paint that needs touching up; open and close the doors and windows to be sure they don't stick; and so on. If something needs fixing, have the contractor do it. Then sit back and start enjoying the fruit of your laborers.

WHEN YOU CAN DO IT YOURSELF
TIPS FROM THE HOSTS OF TV'S "HOMETIME"

As anyone who has ever undertaken a home-improvement project surely knows, the best way to learn how to do it yourself is to watch someone else do it first. That fact largely explains the success of "Hometime," the Minneapolis-based half-hour television show that's carried each week on 317 PBS stations and watched by an estimated five million viewers. In the show's four years on the air, onetime builder and hardware distributor Dean Johnson and cohost JoAnne Liebeler, a high-spirited former TV news editor, have cheerfully demonstrated 83 remodeling projects ranging from enlarging storage space to adding a porch. They also star in the 36 "Hometime" videocassettes sold by mail (800-345-8000; $12.49 each) and at home centers for $9.99. New Money Guide writer Lani Luciano asked Johnson, 38, and Liebeler, 32, for their advice on when it does and doesn't pay to do it yourself.

Which improvements should a homeowner consider doing on his own?

JOHNSON: In general, labor-intensive jobs can save you

thousands of dollars. For instance, virtually anyone can paint and wallpaper, and most people can refinish a wood floor—jobs that you could pay a professional $20 to $40 an hour to do. Hooking up new fixtures to existing plumbing and wiring is easy too, if you pay attention to where everything was originally. Installing completely new plumbing or wiring is more difficult and time consuming, but not impossible.

LIEBELER: Even if the project seems too complicated to try on your own, you can contribute a lot of money-saving labor by simply working along with a professional. For instance, you can hire a landscaper to lay the underground pipes for your lawn sprinkler, but do all the reseeding and camouflage plantings yourself.

What's not worth trying alone?

JOHNSON: Projects that require expensive materials that you can either waste or spoil. For example, laying carpet or installing granite countertops takes the proper tools and an expert to know how to cut and fit economically. And projects that disrupt crucial living space tend to make you sorry you started. You can renovate the extra bathroom in your own sweet time, but racing to put your only bathroom back on line is no pleasure. Actual building work—framing out a new room, adding windows and doors—takes more training and time than most people have, too.

LIEBELER: Also, plastering a ceiling is a miserable job; stuff falls in your face constantly. I don't know how Michelangelo painted the Sistine Chapel, especially if he had to plaster it himself.

Whom can the home handyman call on for assistance?

LIEBELER: You mean besides us? Actually, there are about 50 good remodeling books published by Sunset for $6 to $14 each. If a local building inspector at town hall is friendly, he or she may offer technical advice.

Where do you get the best materials and the best deals?

JOHNSON: At the big home centers. The retail chains buy in such volume that their prices come as close to wholesale as you'll get. And because the quality of their items is standardized, you can be sure of getting materials that will do the job. Also, because home centers are geared to do-ityourselfers rather than to the pros, their products sometimes result in simpler, cheaper ways to do some projects.

Like what?

JOHNSON: There are kits for such things as outdoor lighting, home-security systems, even fireplaces. The kit may not produce the same quality of professional polish as an expert's handiwork, but it may be fine for your needs. For instance, installing a brick fireplace will require a mason and cost at least $5,000. On the other hand, you can put in a prefab metal firebox by yourself for about $1,800.

What would you tell someone who is a little nervous about trying a do-it-yourself project?

JOHNSON: Research what's involved in the project, step by step. Then walk it through in your mind. If you can imagine yourself coping with each task, you'll do fine.

8. The Best Ways to Pay for Remodeling Projects

Carla A. Fried

Before your contractor hammers the first nail, be sure you've shopped shrewdly and pounded out the best deal on your renovation loan.

Picking the ideal loan to bankroll your home-improvement project isn't nearly as much fun as shopping for the perfect whirlpool tub. But to prevent your hard-earned bucks from being drained away by astronomical interest rates or fat loan fees, you must draw the blueprint for your financing before the renovation work begins. For small fix-ups costing $3,000 or less, try to sidestep a loan altogether and pay for the project out of savings. "Even if the interest is tax deductible," says Henrietta Humphreys, a San Francisco financial adviser, "it's far cheaper to avoid interest payments entirely and use cash." But assuming your plans are more ambitious than merely putting a fresh coat of paint in the family room, you will probably need a loan.

Fortunately, now is a terrific time to grab one. Want choices? You've got 'em: home-equity credit lines, standard home-improvement loans, mortgage refinancing, and unsecured personal loans are only a few of your options. Looking for bargains? No sweat. Many banks, savings and loans, and even major brokerage firms are so eager to lend that they are slashing interest rates or waiving fees. Shearson Lehman Hutton Mortgage, for example, charges the usual fees for its home-equity line but promises that you will never pay more than the prime lending rate, recently 10 percent. And if it's tax relief you're after, a smart borrowing strategy can deliver it. (For tax tips, see page 71; for a listing of recent loan rates and fees, see the table on page 73.)

For large loans—such as a $20,000-or-more deal to put a '90s spin on a '50s kitchen—you're usually better off with a so-called secured loan. Example: a home-equity line that taps the equity in your house, which you pledge as collateral. The relatively low interest rates—lately 12 percent, or typically three to four percentage points below those on other renovation loans—and a long repayment period of up to 30 years can keep your monthly payments manageable.

If you bought your first house within the past few years, however, chances are you have little, if any, equity to borrow against. So your only choice may be an unsecured loan. Many lenders will make home-improvement loans of as much as $20,000 even on houses with no equity cushion. And since unsecured loans don't require you to pledge your house as collateral, lengthy title searches and appraisals aren't needed. You can usually count on getting your money within a week, compared with four weeks for a secured loan. The downside: unsecured loans' higher rates and shorter repayment periods dramatically boost monthly payments. For example, the monthly tab on a $20,000, seven-year unsecured home-improvement loan at the recent going rate of 15 percent is $386, versus $221 for a home-equity loan at recent rates repaid over 30 years.

Even if you put up your home as collateral, the actual size of the loan you get ultimately depends on your ability to make monthly payments. As a rule, lenders demand that monthly carrying costs for all your debt not exceed 37 percent of your gross monthly income. So if you monthly salary is $5,000 and you already shell out $1,500 a month for your car loan and mortgage, a bank isn't likely to let you take on more than an additional $350 a month in payments. Thus even if you have $150,000 in home equity, you won't qualify for more than $34,000 on a 30-year loan at 12 percent.

Since interest rates can vary wildly even among the same

types of loans, they should be your first screen for comparing financing deals. You should be particularly wary of lenders dangling super-low teaser rates that get marked up faster than merchandise on Rodeo Drive. For example, Maryland National Bank in Baltimore hawks a home-equity line that starts at 8.9 percent but jumps as much as 2¾ percentage points above prime in three months.

If you find you've fallen for such a come-on, you have an escape hatch. The 1988 Home Equity Loan Consumer Protection Act that went into effect last November lets you back out of an equity-line agreement without losing your application fee up to three days after you apply.

Rates, of course, aren't your only concern. Be sure you also grill the lender about fees. For a secured loan you will usually face much the same closing costs as you would when taking out a mortgage: a $150 to $200 application fee and $300 to $400 for a property appraisal and title search. You may also pay one to three points (each point equals 1 percent of the loan or line). These fees can easily hit $1,000 on a $20,000 home-equity loan. With an unsecured loan, up-front costs are usually limited to a credit-check charge of up to $50.

While you should look for a loan with both low fees and a tantalizing rate, usually a loan has one or the other. If you're borrowing $20,000 or more for 15 years or longer, opt for the better rate. But if you're doing a small project and will pay off the loan quickly, your total costs will be lower if you go for the lowest fees.

Banks and savings and loans stock the widest choice of loan types and terms, but credit unions often have the best deals on home-equity lines. By offering a narrower range of loans than other lenders, credit unions lower their costs and pass the savings along to borrowers. If you don't belong to a credit union, you can snag top home-equity terms by shopping in the month or so before the April tax-filing deadline. Lenders often waive fees then to lure customers who have been 1040'd to death. Don't overlook unconventional sources: Many company 401(k) plans allow you to borrow with no fees and at a rate close to prime. Life insurers usually let you borrow up to 100 percent of the cash value of your life insurance policy. The rate: a soothing 8 percent or less.

To help you choose the loan that suits your project as well as your checkbook, here are details on the most popular financing options:

► **Home-equity line.** The premise behind most equity lines is the same: The lender appraises your house and then lends you up to 80 percent of your equity—that is, the market value of the house minus the mortgage balance. You draw on the variable-rate line by writing checks against a special account the lender sets up or, in some cases, by using a credit card tied to your loan account.

The combination of low rates and the convenience of borrowing by simply writing a check makes these loans ideal for large projects for which you will be paying a contractor over several months to a year. It also slashes your interest costs. With other loans you get your cash in a lump sum and immediately begin paying interest on the entire loan. But with an equity line, says Ken Williams, coauthor of *The Home Equity Survival Guide* (Longman, $14.95), "the interest clock doesn't start ticking until you write a check."

Some lenders offer balloon lines that allow you to pay only interest during the loan's term, then require full payment when the loan comes due, usually in 10 years. Avoid such deals. If the value of your house falls, you may not have enough equity to cover that big balloon payment. You are better off with a line that requires regular principal payments. Under one new arrangement, the lender freezes your line after a set number of years—usually five or 10—and then requires you to pay the balance on the loan over the next five to 10 years.

► **Home-equity loan.** As with an equity line, you are borrowing against the value of your house that exceeds your mortgage balance. But instead of drawing down cash as you need it, the lender gives you a lump sum and you make regular monthly payments, usually over 10 to 30 years. Also, unlike lines, home-equity loans can have a fixed rate, usually set two to three percentage points above prime. Thus, choose one if you want the comfort of knowing exactly what your monthly payments will be.

► **Refinancing your mortgage.** Another way to tap the built-up equity in your home for remodeling is to refinance—that is, take out a new mortgage based on today's higher value of your house and pay off your old mortgage. For example, if your house is worth $125,000 and your mortgage balance is just $60,000, taking out a new mortgage for 80 percent of your home's value would free up $40,000 for renovations after paying off your old mortgage. The hitch:

you pay closing costs of $2,000 to $4,000 on the entire new loan versus $1,500 or less in fees if you take out a $40,000 equity line. Refinance only if you can grab a new mortgage rate at least two percentage points lower than your present one. Otherwise, it will take more than five years of savings from the lower rate to recoup the closing costs.

► **Home-improvement loans.** These loans, which come in secured and unsecured versions, work best for one-shot projects that cost less than $10,000. But the short repayment period of five to seven years makes monthly payments a stiff $233 on a $10,000 five-year loan at 14 percent. If that's too steep, check out Title I home-improvement loans backed by the Federal Housing Administration. You can borrow up to $17,500 and take up to 15 years to pay it off. The longer term lowers monthly payments by roughly 40 percent. Recent rate: 13 to 15 percent (fixed). Title I loans can be used for improvements such as remodeling a bathroom, but not for luxuries like adding a swimming pool. Poll lenders in your area to find one who makes these loans.

► **Unsecured personal loan.** If you need more than the $10,000 maximum for many home-improvement loans but lack the collateral to qualify for an equity line, an unsecured personal loan may be your only option. Drawbacks: you will pay an interest rate six or more points above prime and have but three to five years to pay back the loan. Approvals are quick (usually three days or less). But unless your project is a small one costing $5,000 or less, skip them.

Reporter associate: Frances C. Marshman

TAX TIPS FOR REMODELERS

Looking for a quick, perfectly legal way to slash the interest rate on your renovation loan? Simple. Choose one whose interest payments are fully tax deductible on Schedule A of your 1040 tax form. The benefits are substantial; the effective interest rate on a 12 percent loan drops to 8.6 percent if you're in the 28 percent federal tax bracket, and to 8 percent if you pay the top rate of 33 percent.

To qualify for this perk, however, you must adhere to a few Internal Revenue Service ground rules. First, the loan must be secured by your home—specifically, the lender must record a lien against your home's title. Otherwise, the interest you pay will be considered consumer interest, which is only 10 percent deductible this year; in 1991, zero. Second, the amount of debt on your primary residence and second home combined—including the renovation loan—cannot exceed the fair market value of the houses or $1.1 million, whichever is less. Third, the loan proceeds must be used for a substantial home improvement such as replacing a roof or building an addition. Exception: the IRS allows you to deduct the interest on as much as $100,000 of home-equity debt and use the loan proceeds for any purpose.

If the loan meets these tests, you can also deduct any points the lender charges (each point equals 1 percent of the loan amount). Application, attorney, and appraisal fees are not deductible.

The rules get thorny if you refinance—for example, you take out a new $300,000 mortgage, pay off the $50,000 balance on your old mortgage, and put $50,000 into a renovation job, leaving you with $200,000 in extra cash. You can fully deduct interest on the amount of refinancing proceeds that went to pay off your old mortgage and fund home improvements. Another $100,000 qualifies as home-equity debt; the interest on this is deductible. The rules on consumer interest apply to the remaining amount of money from the refinancing—$100,000 in this case. Points attributable to home improvements can be deducted immediately. The rest must be written off over the term of the loan. You can deduct the remaining points in a lump sum, however, if you sell the house before you repay the loan.

Warning: you may face additional restrictions on interest deductions if you refinance a mortgage taken out before October 13, 1987. In some instances, refinancing may also leave you liable for an irksome levy known as the alternative minimum tax. To avoid unwittingly running afoul of the IRS, check with your accountant before you refinance.

—Teresa Tritch

YOUR TOP CHOICES FOR FIX-UP LOANS

Below are typical terms that lenders offer for renovation loans. To get the top deal, home in on the interest rate, fees, and tax status of the loan. Lines, equity loans, and refinanced mortgages carry the highest fees, but their lower rates make them the best choices for large projects. You should also consider the loan's term or length. You pay more interest on longer loans, but you can lower monthly payments by 40 percent.

Type	Recent rate	Interest Deductibility	Term	Amount (minimum/ maximum)	Fees
Home-equity line	12% (adjustable; maximum rate of 15% to 18%)	100% for proceeds going toward home improvements, provided total debt on primary residence and second home doesn't exceed $1.1 million	5 to 30 years	$5,000/80% of home equity	Zero to $600 plus up to two points
Home-equity loan	13% (fixed); 12% (adjustable; maximum rate of 15% to 18%)	Same as for home-equity line	5 to 30 years	$5,000/80% of home equity	$200 to $600 plus up to three points
Refinanced mortgage	10.3% (fixed); 8.4% (adjustable; 14% maximum rate)	Same as above. Caution: interest on proceeds used to pay old mortgage is fully deductible if that loan was made on or after Oct. 13, 1987. Otherwise, write-off may be subject to limits	30 years	$40,000/80% of home's market value	$600 to $850 plus up to three points
FHA Title I loan	13% to 15% (fixed)	100% if secured by house	5 to 15 years	$1,500/ $17,500	Zero to $1,000
Home-improvement loan	13% to 15% (fixed)	100% if secured by house; if unsecured, 10% this year and zero beginning in 1991	5 to 7 years	$1,000/ $20,000	Zero to $50
Unsecured personal loan	15% to 18% (fixed)	10% this year; zero starting in 1991	3 to 5 years	$1,000/ $25,000	Zero to $50

9. How to Sell Your Home in a Tough Market

Eric Schurenberg

Get real about price, be fanatical about your home's appearance, find a clever broker, and try a little creativity to close the deal.

Tor Krieger knows how it feels to be on the wrong side of the demand curve. The 46-year-old divorced builder put his 10-room Victorian home on the market in San Francisco last September for $525,000—and nothing happened. Incredulous that a prime property in the recently red-hot Bay Area would languish, he reluctantly lowered the price to $499,000. Then $479,000. "I was dragged down kicking and screaming," he says. Still no bites. Meanwhile, in early October, Krieger moved into a new $275,000 house on the outskirts of Santa Rosa, 50 miles north. He finally nabbed a buyer for $475,000, but only after spending $15,000 in mortgage payments and interest on a personal loan to carry both houses for almost five months.

Krieger is not alone. In city after city, the arithmetic of the housing market, long the seller's staunch ally, has changed sides. Kansas City brokers cite a local two-year supply of homes priced at $200,000 or above. In Oklahoma City, still punch-drunk from the oil patch recession, buyers are so scarce that the average house takes more than six months to sell. And in the formerly thriving markets of metropolitan New York City, sellers are getting desperate. Says Staten Island, New York, real estate attorney Michael Manzulli: "Sellers who last year would begrudge you a $1,000 price cut are slashing their prices in $20,000 chunks. I've never seen that in 25 years of practicing."

Yet even in beleaguered markets like these, some homeowners, such as the Kahnkes (see "One Couple That Has Sold with Ease," p. 80), sell without delay or disappointment. They actively take steps to make their homes stand out. Says John Tuccillo, chief economist of the National Association of Realtors: "In buyers' markets, houses aren't sold—they're marketed."

That's why Bruce A. Percelay, a real estate marketing consultant and author of *Packaging Your Home for Profit* (Little, Brown, $12.95), advises learning how to differentiate your "product" in buyers' minds, just as if you were Gillette bringing out a new razor. Some useful tactics, such as sprucing up your home, are time-tested. Others are new or demand special attention in today's soft marketplace: choosing and using a skillful real estate agent or broker, setting a realistic price, and perhaps even offering buyers special come-ons, like a year's prepaid property taxes. Most of all, you have to be willing to work at it. The key strategies:

CHOOSE THE SHARPEST MERCHANT

Find out what it will really take to move your house by hiring a professional marketer—namely, a clever real estate agent. In a softening market, you may be tempted to try to preserve your profits by selling your home yourself and avoiding the agent's commission (typically 6 or 7 percent, but slightly lower in a few spots). That's unwise. A sharp pro will advertise your home expertly, show it skillfully, and mediate deftly with the buyer. Equally important: only agents can list homes on your area's multiple listing service, the publication or computer data base informing other agents and prospective buyers about your house. In many areas, the service is the entry point for buyers in 8 of every 10 sales.

For recommendations of agents, ask neighbors who recently sold homes like yours, and read real estate brokerage office plaques or ads featuring their most recent top sellers. Invite at least three agents to your house for their listing presentations; there they'll spell out their marketing plans and how much they think you can get for your home.

Besides being an irresistible marketer, your agent should know your neighborhood thoroughly and belong to a real estate brokerage with a superb local reputation. If you still can't decide between two otherwise equally qualified agents from different brokerages, lean toward the firm that has more agents in your area. Most agencies encourage their salespeople to show the firm's own listings first so the brokerage won't need to split the commission with a competitor. That could help give your house greater exposure faster. Moreover, odds are that a larger agency will have a fatter advertising budget. In many markets, the dominant brokerages now promote their listings each Sunday on 30-minute daytime television shows—a medium that smaller agencies can rarely afford. Most firms using TV shows try to give each listing a minute or so of air time, usually at no extra cost to the seller.

Once you've selected an agent, tell him or her you want to sign an "exclusive right to sell" listing contract. With this arrangement, the agent collects a commission if the home sells during your listing period, even if *you* actually find the buyer. By promising not to sell the house out from under your agent, you encourage him or her to work as hard on your house as on other listings. Be sure your listing contract has an escape clause that kicks in after no more than 90 days. This way, your agent will know you expect quick action. If the house hasn't sold by then but you are still satisfied with the agent, you can always renew the agreement.

In a sluggish market, don't even suggest amending the contract to slice a few points off the broker's commission. "Look at it from the broker's point of view," says Michael Thomsett, author of *The Complete Guide to Selling Your Home* (Dow Jones–Irwin, $19.95). "Whom would you work harder for: an employer who paid you 6 percent or one who insisted that you take 3 percent?" Similarly, in a cold market, resist the temptation to sign with a discount agency that charges only 3 percent or so. Homes listed with discounters tend to generate low interest among selling brokers, who understandably would rather split 6 percent than 3 percent. Moreover, many cut-rate agencies also require sellers to pay for their own advertising or even show their houses themselves.

In fact, rather than trying to cut commissions, you might consider offering a bonus to the selling agent if the home gets snapped up for, say, 97 percent of the asking price. It could be cash—for example, 1 percent of the selling price in addition to the normal commission—or merchandise, such as a pair of airline tickets to anywhere in the continental U.S. Sound farfetched? Real estate developers and builders offer such incentives regularly.

PRICE IT TO SELL

Perhaps the most common and damaging mistake sellers make in weak markets today is clinging to yesterday's prices. When sales are spotty, what your new neighbors paid for their place last year—or even three months ago—may not be much more relevant to your home's market value than what the Dutch paid for Manhattan. By asking too much initially, you squander the critical first 30 to 45 days of the listing period. Your freshly spiffed-up house will look its best in those early weeks, and it will be shown more, as agents bring by their current stable of shoppers. Lose those buyers and you will have to wait for new prospects to trickle in.

Your agent will suggest an asking price based on recent sales of what he or she considers comparable homes. Pin down the agent. Ask for the addresses of those homes and their sales dates. Then drive by to ensure that the homes are comparable to yours.

Decide on a rock-bottom selling price, then set your initial asking price no more than 3 to 5 percent higher. If possible, come in just under the next lowest multiple of $10,000 (for example, at $149,000 rather than $150,000). Not only is there a psychological difference between the two prices, but since many agents screen homes for buyers by computer—searching for, say, all homes listed for less than $150,000—you are likely to wind up on many more buyers' itineraries.

SPRUCE UP WHAT YOU'VE GOT

The tougher the market, the closer to impeccable your house should be before you list it. "In a buyer's market, there may be 10 homes competing for every buyer," says San Antonio broker George Tucker. "So you have to make sure your house does just that: competes." Major remodeling and landscaping projects usually don't pay, but minor repairs and cosmetic makeovers generally do—in a quicker sale, if not a higher price. For example, in August '89 Robert and Gloria Frankel, a museum director and a schoolteacher, repainted the exterior of their four-bedroom Miami ranch house and replaced the roof. The bill exceeded $10,000, but the house sold in six days for $210,000, only $15,000 less than they asked. Neighboring homes have remained unsold for months.

From the outside, your home must look well cared for and welcoming, two components of the vital first impression brokers call curb appeal. New shrubs and flowers seem to be particularly persuasive. For example, Denver broker Linda Law recalls urging a frustrated home seller to dress up a plain house by putting a tub of geraniums on the front porch. The property, which had been on the market for three months, sold within 30 days. "The buyers asked for only one concession," says Law. "They wanted to keep the geraniums."

Inside your home, concentrate on making rooms look sunny and immaculate. You may be able to give the home a more open feel by putting some furniture in storage. After waiting three months for a bid on their three-bedroom Philadelphia townhouse, Arthur Jones and his wife Mary Nomecos did just that, trucking away a favorite Georgian desk to create more space in the living room. Ten days later, the house sold for $157,000, just 7 percent less than their asking price. "Selling isn't about showing people how you live," says their agent Elizabeth Caulk. "It's about show biz."

Overall, your goal should be to make it as easy as possible for potential buyers to imagine themselves living in your house. When buyers have an abundance of choices, as they do in soft markets, they tend to look for reasons to cross homes off their lists. So if your interiors include a lot of personal decorating flourishes, make them over in conservative schemes. "People look for 'vanilla' houses," says Cindy Kanipe, a resale specialist with PHH Homequity in Loveland, Ohio. "Beige carpeting and off-white walls will give you the broadest appeal."

CREATE A PACKAGE THAT STANDS OUT

Remember that promotions work best when they are pitched to the right customers. If you have what might be considered a smallish starter home, consider enticing cash-strapped buyers with an offer to pick up part of their closing costs. To help a buyer qualify for a mortgage, you could float the idea of a mortgage buy-down, in which you pay a lender a flat sum to lower the interest rate on the buyer's mortgage for the first few years. On a 30-year, $100,000 mortgage, it might cost you $2,636 to lower the rate from 10.5 to 8.5 percent for the first year and 9.5 percent for the second, reducing the buyer's monthly payment by $146 to $769. Chicago's MidAmerica Federal Savings Bank offers current mortgage customers a deal it calls "Mortgage Perk." If you move and finance your new home through MidAmerica, the bank will deduct half a point from the loan-origination fee on your new mortgage—and offer the same break on your buyer's loan.

Trade-up buyers, who can often count on sacks of cash from the sale of their previous home, tend to be less impressed by financing incentives. For these buyers, you might consider throwing in a $1,000 redecorating or landscaping allowance or a year's prepaid lawn maintenance service. Diane Mendels, who markets homes in Houston for the nationwide Prudential Relocation Management Services, sometimes offers to pay first-year country club membership fees of $2,500 or so to draw buyers to slow-selling upscale homes.

Even the most creative promotions will be useless if buyers don't know about them, so make sure that the word gets out to both agents and potential buyers. For example, you might encourage your agent to hold an open house for other real estate brokerages before officially putting the house on the market. Give the invited brokers a reason to visit. The enticement could be as simple as hors d'oeuvres and wine in the kitchen or as corny as a drawing for, say, a frozen turkey. "The prize doesn't have to be expensive," says Cindy Kanipe. "You just want to get agents through the door."

To help get the word out to buyers, target your advertising. If you have a starter home, for example, leave leaflets at a nearby rental complex where young couples may be waiting to make the leap to ownership. If your intended buyer is more affluent, mail a description of your home to local corporations' human resources directors, who will know of executives transferring in.

RETHINK YOUR SALES STRATEGY

Monitor the progress of your sales campaign by getting updates from your broker after every showing. Find out what objections prospects are voicing and adapt your strategy accordingly. For example, if buyers seem to prefer newer houses than yours, consider spending $300 or so on a homeowners warranty. Sold through most real estate agencies, such warranties often pay for repairing a house's air-conditioning, heating, or plumbing system in the first year of occupancy. Whenever you cut your price sharply or alter your selling strategy in any major way, have your agent relist the home with the multiple listing service. The repackaging may induce brokers to give your house a second look.

If your home hasn't sold in three months, it may be time for a new broker. Warning signs: your house is not attracting much buyer traffic, the agent does not keep you regularly informed of prospects' reactions, or he or she is slow to return your calls. Give your broker a chance to explain the situation. But if you're unimpressed, search for another.

If nothing seems to work, you may be tempted to grab a home purchase plan. Some 80 percent of large firms offer such programs to transferees. The company typically agrees to buy your home for the average of two appraisals—one paid by you and one by your firm. The employer—or a relocation company it hires—then sells the house. Some real estate agencies and developers offer similar promotions. Resist them. You could pay a stiff price for their bailouts. For example, some builders try coaxing sellers into buying languishing units by offering to purchase their old homes at only 70 to 90 percent of the appraised value. The developer may further cover his risk by charging top dollar for your new home.

A last resort may be to put your house up for auction (see page 17). This does not eliminate the need for sprucing up the place as you would if you were selling conventionally. Says Steven Burtar, director of client relations for PHH Homequity in Oak Brook, Illinois: "Even in a tough market, if you spend the time and money on marketing up front, you almost always save time and money in the end."

ONE COUPLE THAT HAS SOLD WITH EASE

While others suffered through home-selling sob stories, Jerome and J.R. (Jan Ruth) Kahnke of St. Paul have made three smooth Twin Cities sales since 1984, trading both up and down for maximum profits. In fact, when the Kahnkes sold their 1,500-square-foot, three-bedroom Tudor in St. Paul last winter for $97,000 and traded up to a more luxurious $186,500, 2,400-square-foot, four-bedroom colonial nearby, they were a little surprised that the whole process, from listing to contract, took a full two weeks. After all, selling a house had never taken the couple that *long* before.

True, the steady local real estate market didn't hurt. Prices in the Kahnkes' neighborhoods have risen about 4 percent a year on average since 1984. Most of the couple's success, though, springs from the way they methodically planned each sale, practically from the day they bought. "We're 'tomorrow' people," explains Jerome, 34, a product liability lawyer. "We're always thinking ahead, always dreaming." As homeowners, that means making their house as livable and salable as possible.

Smooth sale-ing for the Kahnkes (and kids Taylor, 4, and Mackenzie, 16 months) has meant using four strategies: fixing up a few key rooms; knowing when to sell; ferreting out data about the neighborhood to attract would-be buyers; and using the right agent. The details:

The Kahnkes believe that a home's kitchen and master bath/bedroom can make or break a sale. Says Jerome: "If you can make those two rooms seem appealing, you've taken the downside totally out of the picture." When the Kahnkes bought their Tudor in July 1987 for $86,000, they noticed that an oversize refrigerator, portable dishwasher, and mud-brown cabinets made the tight 11-foot-by-15½-foot kitchen seem even more compact. In five days, Jerome and J.R., 35, installed a smaller refrigerator, a built-in dishwasher, and a light fixture, and painted the cabinets off-white. Total cost: about $850. The Kahnkes also recognized that an 18-foot-by-22-foot upstairs bedroom had untapped potential: enough unused territory for both a walk-in closet and a bath. So J.R. sketched out plans for a closet and then built it with her husband for about $100 in materials. "We both love working with our hands," she says. "It gives us a real sense of accomplishment." Her plans for a master bath were ready when they sold the house in February 1989, just 12 days after listing it at $97,000.

The couple also pays close attention to smaller details before putting a house on the market. That means eliminating distractions that can turn off buyers, such as doorknobs that don't turn and floors that creak (which they fix with adhesive or nails). Likewise, they advise against fighting a home's style by, say, laying an orange shag carpet in a Victorian home.

Like the famed Paul Masson winery, the Kahnkes will sell no house before its time. Jerome watches mortgage rates for clues. He knows that when rates rise, buyers turn skittish and big houses especially become tougher to market; when rates drop, larger homes get snapped up more quickly. Consequently, the Kahnkes waited from December 1984 until June 1986, when rates had fallen from roughly 13 to 10 percent, before unloading the nine-bedroom, turn-of-the-century mansion they had bought in St. Paul's prestigious Crocus Hill district. Eager to trade down to a home demanding less upkeep and thus allow for more time with the newborn Taylor, they sold the place for $194,000. That was $42,000 more than they paid—a gain of $36,000 after inflation and the $4,500 they spent on home repairs.

The Kahnkes and their real estate agent, John Hayes of Merrill Lynch Realty, also typically research their neighborhood for information they can present in the best light to prospective buyers. They suggest, for instance, that homeowners near an airport call the terminal to check flight frequencies; such data can allay a potential buyer's worries about airplane noise.

Even though the Kahnkes don't expect to move soon, they are plotting sale number four. The first steps will be enlarging their kitchen by about 60 percent and adding on an 11-foot-by-14-foot master bathroom with a Jacuzzi. The vagaries of the mortgage market will take it from there.

—Ira Hellman

TAX TIPS FOR SELLERS

Selling your house can provide the biggest tax break of your life: You may be able to defer the taxes on your profit for years or even avoid *ever* paying them. The trick is understanding how the IRS calculates house-sale gains. The basics:

You can snatch a once-in-a-lifetime *exclusion* from taxes on as much as $125,000 in capital gains—$62,500 if you're married and file separately—if (1) you are 55 or older and (2) have owned the house and lived in it as your principal residence for at least three of the past five years. If you and your spouse file jointly, only one of you must meet the tests to claim the exclusion.

A seller who doesn't qualify for the exclusion but is buying another principal residence usually gets a *tax deferral* of his gains. The two IRS hurdles: (1) you must buy or build the new house within two years before or after the sale and (2) your new house must cost at least as much as the so-called adjusted sales price of your old one.

The second stipulation is trickier than it seems. You may incorrectly assume that if you bought a house for, say, $80,000 and will now sell it for $125,000, you have a $45,000 capital gain and must therefore buy a home for $125,000 or more to defer the taxes on it. Actually, as the worksheet on page 84 shows, to calculate the gain accurately, you have to factor in such things as closing costs and home improvements. Fortunately, the extra pencil pushing can help slash your taxes. In the prior example, if you had spent $8,000 on improvements to the original house, you could knock down your capital gain at least to $37,000 ($45,000 minus $8,000).

Naturally enough, all sales require some IRS paperwork. If you will claim the $125,000 exclusion, or defer the taxes on your sale, or have a loss, file Form 2119. Taxable gains must be reported on Schedule D.

Should you die before paying taxes on your deferred gains, your house will become part of your estate. Then any federal estate or state death taxes due will depend on the overall value of your assets. If they total $600,000 or less, your estate won't owe federal taxes. Many states have lower cutoffs. New York, for instance, taxes estates above $108,000.

—Teresa Tritch

CALCULATING YOUR GAIN

Use this worksheet to figure out how much, if any, of your house-sale profits will be taxed and how much of any capital gain you must defer. If you claimed a home-office deduction over the years, fine-tune the numbers with your tax preparer so they will reflect the percentages of your house allocated to residential and business uses. The worksheet presumes you meet the tests for deferring gains discussed in "Tax Tips for Seller."

1. **Sales price** ________
2. **Selling expenses** (including broker's commission and legal fees) ________
3. **Net sales proceeds** (line 1 minus line 2) ________
4. **Net investment in the home you're selling**
   - **a.** Purchase price plus nondeductible closing costs ________
   - **b.** Cost of improvements ________
   - **c.** Add lines 4a and 4b ________
   - **d.** Deferred gain, if any, from previous home sales ________
   - **e.** Insurance reimbursements for casualty losses ________
   - **f.** Tax write-offs for casualty losses ________
   - **g.** Residential energy credits claimed through 1985 ________
   - **h.** Add lines 4d through 4g ________
   - **i.** Line 4c minus line 4h ________
5. **Your capital gain** (line 3 minus line 4i) If zero or less, stop here. You have no gain or a nondeductible loss ________
6. **One-time exclusion** If you elect the one-time tax exclusion for a seller age 55 or older, enter the amount on line 5 or $125,000, whichever is less, and continue to line 7. If not, enter zero and skip to line 8 ________
7. **Adjusted capital gain** (line 5 minus line 6) If the result is zero or less, stop. You owe no tax. If the result is greater than zero, you owe taxes on this amount unless you are buying another principal residence. In that case, move on to the next steps to see how much tax you can defer on the gain ________
8. **Fix-up expenses on the home you're selling** Enter the cost of repairs you make within 90 days of signing a sales contract and pay for within 30 days after the sale ________
9. **Adjusted sales price** (line 3 minus line 8) ________
10. **Cost of new home** (down payment, mortgage, and closing costs) ________
11. **Taxable gain** (line 9 minus the total of line 10 plus line 6) If the result is zero or less, enter zero and proceed to line 12. If it is greater than zero, enter that amount, or the figure on line 5, or—if you elected the exclusion—the number on line 7, whichever is less ________
12. **Amount of capital gain you must defer** (line 5 minus line 11 or, if you elected the exclusion, line 7 minus line 11) ________

HOW NOT TO CARRY TWO HOMES

What's worse than being stuck with a home in a slow market? Getting caught with two. Few families can sustain carrying costs on two houses for long, yet brokers estimate that about one in four home buyers risks that kind of squeeze by purchasing a new place before unloading his old one. It almost always makes sense to sell first, particularly in sluggish markets, where homes can languish for months. Asserts Cincinnati broker Stephen Casper: "In a soft market, you shouldn't even shop for a new house until you have a firm contract of sale on your current one."

Instead, use the time that your present home is up for sale not only to investigate neighborhoods but also to line up financing. Many lenders will pre-approve you for a mortgage of a stipulated amount even before you start house shopping. The advantage is that once you do sell, you can find a new home and close on it quickly. To give yourself extra time for house hunting, try negotiating with your buyer to schedule the closing in 90 to 120 days rather than the normal 60 to 90 days.

Before signing a contract on the new house, make sure you won't be blind-sided if the sale on your old one falls through. Pay a professional inspector $150 to $300 to check out your home before you list it and repair any surprises that turn up. Also, make sure your agent has ascertained that a prospective buyer will qualify for financing before showing him your home.

If your only nibble is from someone who will buy once he sells his own place, write a "seller's contingency" or "kick-out" clause into the sales contract. This lets you keep showing your house even after you've accepted his offer. Then, should another purchaser come along, would-be buyer number one will have two or three days either to waive his contingency or to withdraw the bid.

Now, assume the worst. Despite your precautions, you find yourself forced to close on a house with no buyer in sight for your current one. Don't try to sell your house vacant. Without furniture, a house's minor flaws tend to be more obvious. In addition, buyers often have trouble envisioning what an unoccupied house would look like furnished.

If you can handle the headaches of landlording, you

might rent the house as you continue to show it. Ideally, you'll lease the house with an option to buy—the tenant pays you a rent that's 10 to 20 percent above the market for, say, a year or two and gets the right to buy the house at a predetermined price anytime during that period. If he buys, the extra rent counts toward the down payment; if not, you keep the money.

Another alternative is hiring a home-sitting agency to move in until you sell. At no cost to you, two large regional agencies, Showhomes of America (214-243-1900) in Texas and Caretakers of America (303-233-2676) in Colorado screen home sitters, generally students or transferring employees. In return for rents that might be 75 percent below the market rate, the sitters furnish the property, maintain it, pay utilities, and vacate at 10 days' notice. Keep in touch with your broker to make sure the house is well cared for.

—E.S.

---

10. The Special Meaning of a House

Augustin Hedberg

"There's an American with a house about five miles up the road. You can just stay there, eh," said the hitchhiker with the banjo and the snake wrapped around his waist as he got into my car along a particularly lonesome stretch of the Trans-Canada highway in 1970. The invitation to stay at the house was a generous one, made by one itinerant to a person he surely thought was another, and I picked up on it instantly, since the house that he was referring to was actually mine.

I had bought the place for cash at the age of 24, using the $2,200 I had saved from swinging a mop as an attendant in a New Jersey mental institution. It was a 10-room wreck and came with what turned out to be 11 pickup-truck loads of empty green wine bottles scattered within spitting distance of the back stoop. The man I bought it from, a reformed alcoholic, took my money and drove straight to the liquor store, where he bought two cases of Moosehead. "Here, these come with the house," he said, as he bounced them into the back seat of my 1962 Volvo 544 coupe. I spent the next two years slapping up Sheetrock, slapping down shingles, and slapping myself in the face wondering what in hell I was doing. I'm still not sure, except that in the afterglow of the '60s it seemed that anything worth doing was worth doing wrong.

If pressed back then, I would probably have said that I was looking for the meaning of life. Now, glancing back over the decades and smoking chimneys of my two other houses, I must say that in some ways I found meaning—or at least a small and exceedingly bourgeois part of it: houses are holy. They are the material anchors that secure our ephemeral souls. We are the creatures without fur, or shell, or scale, or feather, whose lot it is to spend our days carpeting, clapboarding, and curtaining the space around us. Set a man on the moon with a pile of rocks, come back in a week, and he will have started a house.

My second house, if not on the moon itself, was certainly under its influence. It flooded with tidal precision. This, as any homeowner who has peered down the stairs into a glassy surface of water could attest, is not uncommon, particularly in the swampy suburbs around Washington, D.C., where I lived. Like young Egyptians contemplating the flooding of the Nile, my children grew up imagining that some unseen deity caused the transformation of their warm, dry world into a lake each spring. Neither ritual incantations nor the intervention of larcenous contractors could stem the flood. A three-horsepower Sears Wet-Dry Vac could drain the three-inch-deep pool, but the pleasure of seeing our possessions reappear as the waterline dropped was dampened by—well, was just dampened. We sold the house in the dead of winter and moved to Pennsylvania.

FOUR-BEDROOM colonial on large lot. 2½ baths. Attached garage. Perfect for you.

So read the ad. And so it was. Stately, distinctive, and glowing, this house (price: $103,000) consumed my every waking moment, and most of my paycheck as well. I shot out of bed on Saturday mornings with the muzzle velocity of a one-man fire department and set to a thousand tasks. Let's see . . . I converted the garage to a library, moved the driveway to the edge of the lot, installed a wood stove and flue, laid a sweeping flagstone walkway to the front door, and learned the internal anatomy of every appliance in the house to the point that I could identify each by the smell of its grease.

What happened? Ah, the hitchhiker was wrong; you can't just stay there. My wife is asking for the house and child support.

Ours is a containerized journey. We begin in the womb, end in a casket, and in between inhabit a house. About the first and last we have little say, but the house is what we make of it: our best investment and, whether we intend it or not, a reflection of our own personalities. "We live here," says Oliver Rose about his beloved house, the *real* star of the hit movie *The War of the Roses*. Responds his wife Barbara: "*This* is who we are?"